Praise for *Sex and the Soul of a Woman*

In our sex-crazed society, *Sex and the Soul of a Woman* elevates both sex and womanhood. Paula Rinehart gives hope and healing and shows practically how to internalize boundaries. We highly recommend this spiritually thought-provoking book.

—Linda Dillow and Lorraine Pintus,
authors of *Intimate Issues* and *Giftwrapped by God*

Finally, a fresh, modern book that allows a woman to fully understand the impact of a sexual relationship. If we could have learned earlier the worth we bring to men, instead of the shame we often bring into our lives, many of our wounds could have been avoided. If I could pick one book for every woman I know to read, regardless of her background, it would be *Sex and the Soul of a Woman*.

—Jamie, Grand Rapids, Michigan

I saw myself throughout the pages of this book—big-time! It helped for someone to validate my feelings of regret and loss during the time of my life that included one relationship after another with men. It's the book I wish someone had put in my hands then.

—Fran, Costa Mesa, California

So many of us know that sexual intimacy outside of marriage is a cheapened form, at best. What we often don't know is the most freeing and life-giving part—the why. This book offers hope and meaning in an arena where we sometimes doubt the goodness of God. Never before has my sexual dependence on God struck me so hard. Without him, all I have to offer a man is an act.

—Stephanie, Washington, D.C.

It was refreshing for me to be affirmed in the value of sexual innocence. I'm comforted to realize that God has placed boundaries around sexuality because of our tremendous importance to him.

—Carolyn, Calgary, Alberta, Canada

I'm a well-educated twenty-two-year-old woman, and this is the first time I've heard some of the ideas put forth in this book. It helped me most by making me think about "God being inside sex." The whole book made me think about romance and sex differently.

—Jena, Roanoke, Virginia

Paula Rinehart unmasks the myth that nonmarital sex is harmless. She carefully undresses a woman's pain to reveal the scarred soul that lies beneath the illusion that sexual intimacy is merely a physical act. But she doesn't leave bare this reality. She redresses it by sensitively detailing God's intent for married sex. A woman who wants to experience spiritual and emotional wholeness is gently led back to the path of purity to walk in the freedom ushered in by God-esteem, dignity, and self-respect.

—LaVerne Tolbert, author of
Keeping Your Kids Sexually Pure

Sex AND THE Soul OF A Woman

The Reality of Love & Romance in an Age of Casual Sex

Paula Rinehart

ZONDERVAN™

GRAND RAPIDS, MICHIGAN 49530 USA

ZONDERVAN™

Sex and the Soul of a Woman
Copyright © 2004 by Paula Rinehart

Requests for information should be addressed to:

Zondervan, *Grand Rapids, Michigan 49530*

Library of Congress Cataloging-in-Publication Data

Rinehart, Paula.
     Sex and the soul of a woman : the reality of love and romance in an age
of casual sex / Paula Rinehart.
        p. cm.
     Includes bibliographical references.
     ISBN 0-310-25220-2
     1. Sex—Religious aspects—Christianity.   2. Christian women—
Religious life.   I. Title.
     BT708.R49 2004
     241'.66—dc22

                                                    2003022096

Published in association with the literary agency of Alive Communications, Inc., 7680 Goddard Street, Suite 200, Colorado Springs, CO 80920.

Interior design by Michelle Espinoza

Printed in the United States of America

04 05 06 07 08 09 10 /❖ DC/ 10 9 8 7 6 5 4 3 2 1

To my father, Ralph Corn,
my husband, Stacy,
and our son, Brady—
three good men especially dear to me

Contents

Preface

I trust you chose this book because you recognize the vital connection between your soul and your sexuality. Perhaps you have concerns about the sexual landscape between men and women. Or maybe you have hurts and regrets, as well as hopes and dreams, to which this book might put words.

As you read, I hope you will feel that you are in the midst of a spirited conversation about where relationships with men are meant to lead and what roles sex and sexuality are meant to play in your life. I'd like this book to seem like a companion on a journey. If promiscuity has played a part in your life, this book offers a door to something better—to the fulfillment of even deeper longings.

The book has grown out of hours and hours of listening to women tell their stories—stories you will recognize as coming from many women you know, or even from yourself. As I have listened to woman after woman describe the impact on her life of broken sexual bonds, I have been struck by how much of her real self a woman loses in this experience—often at an age before she even begins to come into her own. It's like seeing a house with the lights on inside, but the windows all boarded up. So little light—life—shines out from within. Being parceled out sexually to too many men takes a toll on the spirit.

When I listen to such stories, I sense a tiny sliver of the grief God feels—the God who created woman in his own image, with life-giving potential. Yet while I sense God's grief, I also gain fresh appreciation for the power of Jesus Christ and the wonder of the gospel to restore our broken, sinful selves. I am reminded of Jesus' words: "Very truly I tell you, everyone who sins is a slave to sin. Now a slave has no permanent place in the family, but a son belongs to it forever. So if the Son sets you free, you will be free indeed."[1] Ultimately, only the One who made us can set us free.

This book is not an effort to reengineer the old order, like some Gentile equivalent of *Fiddler on the Roof* with me singing, "Tradition, tradition, tradition" throughout its pages. Every age has its glory—and its shameful lies. My desire is simply that we look into the essence of our sexuality—male and female—and listen to God speaking at the core of our being.

So, welcome. Fasten your seat belt. I think you will find this a good ride, an insightful journey, a helpful process, and maybe even a new beginning.

Paula Rinehart,
August 2003

Sex is responsible for most of the ecstasies on the planet, but it is also responsible for lots of murders and suicides. It is the most powerful of all fires, the most dangerous of all fires, and the fire which, ultimately, lies at the base of everything, including the spiritual life.

Ronald Rolheiser

Chapter 1

A Rose Every Friday

Our society is filled with people for whom the sexual relationship is one where body meets body but where person fails to meet person.... The result is that [relationships] lead not to fulfillment but to a half-conscious sense of incompleteness, of inner loneliness, which is so much the sickness of our time.

Frederick Buechner

*C*arol gathers her clothes off the floor, tiptoeing silently around the bedroom in the early dawn, hoping not to wake this man. Snoring in quiet, even rhythm, it will be hours before he gets up. When he can, he likes to sleep until noon, and she has a ton of stuff to do today. Besides, it's easier to slip back into her place before her roommates awaken—fewer raised eyebrows and sly smiles to contend with that way.

Driving back to her apartment, Carol muses over how their relationship began. Who ever would have thought that cochairing a political committee would lead to this? They began as good friends, challenging each other's opinions with an occasional lighthearted jab. But one thing led to another, and after a few months, she began to stay over at his place. It made for less hassle. How or when or where the relationship turned sexual, she isn't sure. She just knows that she is starting to have feelings for this guy, and that this could be a problem.

There are no guarantees in relationships now. How many times have her friends drilled that into her? "You just have to go with the flow" is the mantra she hears. "Don't say much; don't ask for anything. Just play it cool and see where the relationship goes."

The problem is that Carol has already done this twice before.

Something cataclysmic is happening in the sexual lives of women today. A breathtaking amount of change in the way men and women relate to each other has taken place in one short generation. The great mating dance that was repeated for centuries has been shortened dramatically. A man and a woman fall into bed now with no promises made and no expectations to which they can hold each other. Love and romance take a backseat to the more immediate pleasures of sex, which, in its many forms, can be experienced with no immediately apparent effect on the invisible world of soul and spirit. I doubt that even Aldous Huxley would recognize the brave new sexual world we inhabit.

A man and a woman fall into bed now with no promises made and no expectations to which they can hold each other.

As a counselor invited into the inner sanctum of one woman's life after another, I have the privilege of entering women's lives and hearing their stories. It is a unique perch from which to observe the monumental changes taking place. Women from every background—in college and in emerging careers—talk about the challenges they face in a world where the vintage road maps between men and women seem as though they were drawn in fading ink.

In many ways, of course, regardless of age or background, we all are telling the same story—of losses that are difficult to absorb, fears that keep us awake at night, and dreams that have been incubating in us since we were quite small. But a new common denominator exists now—in the lives of younger women especially—a different narrative thread repeated in endless variation. Women's lives are being shaped by a culture with a sexuality gone mad. Women are paying a tremendous price for the loosening of sexual boundaries—in broken hearts, in lost time, in confused sense of self. Perhaps these voices are recognizable:

- Shannon is desperate for something that will curb the panic attacks that descend on her unannounced. Her job as a news reporter is being threatened by these sweaty emotional monsters. Shannon has just broken up with a man named Ben—a great guy she met last year in college and followed to the city, where they both landed their first jobs. She feels bad about beginning to sleep with Ben a few years ago. It violated her convictions as a Christian, but she developed her own way of justifying their sexual relationship. At least it was better than so many women around her. This was no one-night fling—she and Ben were planning a future together.

  Two things caught Shannon by surprise. She hadn't anticipated that her growing attachment to Ben would be met with a reaction of his own—she was slowly caricatured as this woman "with too much of a hold on him." The more attached she became, the more detached he got—until she finally wanted out altogether. And Shannon had no idea that leaving Ben after this investment of herself would feel like a miniature divorce.

- Donna says she has always been sexually curious. Movies she saw in middle school, stories of her older siblings' late-night capers, and easy access to soft porn left her primed for her own sexual adventures. When a boy showed interest in her, it was she who upped the ante, moving things to the next level of sexual intimacy. By the time she left high school, she had been with a good number of guys.

Now, in her second year of college, Donna finally has begun to wonder where her sexual activity is headed. *What is the point?* she asks. Why does she feel numb inside—as though her body is disconnected from the rest of her? Donna watches other couples and wonders if she will ever know what it feels like to have a man love her—just for her. A vague sense of regret and loss she cannot name follows her around. She longs to retrace her steps and find the innocence of soul she once knew.

- Emily's introduction to her own sexuality came from the most injurious of all possible routes. Her favorite brother used to slip into her room at night, just as she was turning twelve, where he held her in his arms and fondled her changing body. The bittersweet experience of hating yourself while you enjoyed intimacy never meant to be was profoundly ingrained in Emily's psyche. Being date-raped in high school just seemed like one more act in a bad play. With the sexual walls in her life broken down, Emily accepted the terms of the inevitable: a relationship with a man comes with a sexual price tag. Sex is part of the dues you pay to keep the relationship—and she has had quite a few of those. The fog and pain after each breakup leads to one poor choice in men after another.

Emily feels as though she steps in and out of two lives. On Sunday mornings she plays the flute in a worship ensemble. She sincerely wants to follow God, but her sexual life feels out of her control. She can't reconcile her lifestyle with her beliefs about God.

In any direction you turn now, women feel not just the opportunity, but the pressure, to be sexual. I am sure the checkout lane in your grocery store looks just like mine. On any given day, I can reach for at least two magazines that will give me the latest tip on how to "do" a man—as though sex is assumed between two mature adults, as though it is a woman's job to provide the best experience possible, as though a woman should be able to shield her heart while she bares her body on cue. Although in the Christian community we subscribe to a different vision, we find ourselves swimming in the same cultural soup. We cannot help but be affected.

I hear similar stories in any part of the country. When I give a seminar to college women or single women in the marketplace almost anywhere, they say

In any direction you turn now, women feel not just the opportunity, but the pressure, to be sexual.

the same things. "I was swept into major sexual experiences early on, before I even knew what was happening." Women often feel like they've sexually traded little bits of their soul they can't get back. "I was so afraid I'd lose this guy that I felt like I had to have sex with him." It's hard to hold a line when a woman feels like a guy can get what he wants from three other women if she refuses.

Not every trend concerning women's sexuality has been negative, however. Some changes deserve a round of applause—the validation of a woman's experience of sexual pleasure, the insistence that a woman's life is her own, given to her by God, and not defined solely by her attachment to a man. These truths are timeless. But the sexual revolution that my generation ushered through the door has taken us way beyond both—and far down a costly path.

"Revolutions" are supposed to usher in a braver, better world. Why, then, are women not happier than they seem to be?

This strange lack of happiness is being articulated now by a small cache of young female writers—savvy, intelligent, brutally honest women who wonder out loud why their peers, liberated from all the constraints of previous generations, do not seem to be prospering as expected. One particularly fresh voice with a daring message belongs to Wendy Shalit, an orthodox Jewish writer, who openly began to challenge the ease with which men and women get intimate. While a student at Williams College, she exposed the absurdity of men and women trying to share the same bathroom facilities, as though their physical differences could be neutralized. Soon after graduation she wrote the best-selling book *A Return to Modesty*, essentially pleading with other women to consider the physical and emotional cost of the loss of romance and courtship. She calls what is happening among younger women today "an invisible American tragedy."[2] Her words are not too strong.

While there is indeed much promise in this generation of women, there is also an incredible amount of pain, especially pain that is rooted in mistaken sexual choices. The carnage of the sexual revolution blows into counseling offices like mine with great regularity—women who have so much going for them but who have sustained blows like one-night stands, abortions, and deep bonds with men they must find a way to dig out of the soil of their hearts.

Over and over I am struck with a desire to gather these women and bring them home with me. I want to pour them a cup of tea and invite them to talk. As a woman born in another era (when bell bottoms were popular the first time) and having slept with one and the same man for thirty years, I think this is a hard time to be female. It is true that nearly every conceivable door of opportunity is open to women now, but there is scarcely anyone standing in front of some of these doors and saying the obvious: *This path does not lead to a life you want.*

A Longing for Romance

In survey after survey, women insist that, while they value having more options in how they relate to men, they miss the sense of romance, of being pursued by a man. There seems to be a growing awareness that something beautiful between men and women is being trampled in the rush to the sexual. Some call it "lost civility." The notion that a woman is a prize in her own right, worth crossing the dance floor of life to get to know deeply, is no longer assumed. Indeed, the "death of romance" we are experiencing now has become a universal moan among women.

There seems to be a growing awareness that something beautiful between men and women is being trampled in the rush to the sexual.

In researching this book, I also interviewed women from earlier eras—ones who danced the night away to the music of a twenty-piece band or who kept love going in wartime through letters to a soldier half a world away. Their stories are almost lost to us now. Theirs was not an easy time, either, for they faced pressures of a different sort. Their options in life were notoriously limited. Becoming a wife and a mother was invariably the next step in a scripted life that presented far fewer choices.

Yet there was a beauty and an elegance to their relationships with men that one too rarely sees these days. Fraternities from the state university, for example, held their annual spring galas at the beach. Men in tuxedos and women in beautiful ball gowns really did dance the night away in a ballroom overlooking the sea—because both parties knew they would retire to separate quarters before the morning dawned. So much more was required of a man. He actually expected to have to court a woman's affection—sometimes riding the train for the day to see her for a few hours, expecting nothing more sexual than a kiss. When a man took a woman out, her care and her good time were his responsibility.

Perhaps the most engaging story that came my way, though, sheds some light on the respect and gentleness men and women tended to offer each other even if they never married. Charlotte, a lovely, silver-haired woman in her seventies, told me how she fell in love with a man she met on a slow boat to Europe while she was in college. They had hours to talk, watching the way the stars shine when there is only sky and sea. Frank continued to write after she returned home; he even came to see her once or twice. But she knew, as she had always known, that she would marry Joe, a man in her hometown whom she had dated for a couple of years. When Charlotte married a year later, out of kindness she sent Frank an invitation to the wedding. He replied with a gift—a leather-bound, early edition of John Milton's classic, his calling card tellingly stuck between the pages of *Paradise Lost*.

We can't turn back the clock, and our current problems would not evaporate even if we could. There are flies in the ointment of love in every day and time. The chastity of women in days gone by was rarely a reflection of real virtue or the thoughtful consideration of sexual ethics. Good girls didn't have sex—it was about that simple. The fear of pregnancy kept many women chaste. Thus, they did not have to do the hard work that women do now of wrestling with the spiritual and emotional implications of joining one's body to another.

I share their stories as a way of gauging how far we have come in a relatively short span of time. "You've come a long way, baby" was the slogan that made Virginia Slims cigarettes famous. Indeed, we have come a long way. The question we must ask ourselves is, when it comes to relating to men, is this where we want to be?

In every generation, we must reach for truth that is time-less—that goes back further than any of us can remember. The only way to construct a life we can live inside is to build on something more solid than ourselves.

Opening Pandora's Box

The dance between men and women was carefully scripted until the late 1960s, when my generation discovered sex—as though it were some recent invention. I have friends who passed through college before sexual restraints broke loose, and their stories sound almost quaint by comparison. They speak of fra-ternity parties where men were required to appear in ties and dress shirts, weekday curfews of 10:00 p.m., and housemothers who ensured that no man ever saw more than the foyer of female living quarters. Two friends, Bill and Sis, dated for two years at the University of North Carolina amid ancient magno-lias and tall stately columns that have served as the backdrop for two hundred years of emerging romances. Every Friday Bill brought Sis a single red rose.

By the late 1960s, this picture was speeding past in the rearview mirror. While protesting the war in Vietnam and burning our bras, our generation also flung open the door of sexual restraint. It was as though we thought we had invented sex. C. S. Lewis once remarked that sex was such a sublime experience—who would ever guess it produced babies? For the first time in history, it didn't. A woman could take a pill, and her worries of getting pregnant were next to nil. The consequences of sleeping together did not arrive in nine months wrapped in a soft blanket, crying for his mama. Other consequences were present, of course—but they went underground, deep into the realm of soul and spirit, where the damage is much harder to calculate.

For as long as there had been wedding vows, sexual intimacy had been something set apart, sacramental, reserved for the realm of lifelong commitment between a man and a woman. Not so for my generation. Inside the room of the sexually initiated was where all the happy people lived—or so they said. And happiness was our big demand. We pushed until we cracked open a door bolted shut for good reason. Those who follow now rush headlong as though the door no longer exists. Inside this room there is pleasure, to be sure. But there is also a cache of sexually transmitted diseases and a truckload of heartache. The truth is that my generation owes the following generations an apology—a profound one.

People have been sleeping around, in and out of the wrong beds, since the dawn of time. The difference is that they knew to blush. When I pledged a college sorority in the 1960s, plenty of girls slept around and no one would pretend otherwise. But that behavior was discreet and accompanied by guilt and shame. My daughter pledged the same sorority twenty-five years later. Her virginity was so distinctive that her sorority sisters nicknamed her "Mary," as in the mother of Jesus. (She is blessed, thankfully, with a fairly thick skin.)

Campus life, almost anywhere now, has become a four-year immersion experience in every nuance of sexual freedom. A woman can't act shocked when a man in a towel emerges from her roommate's door—nor question why it might be a different guy than the one two weeks before. The stereotype of a well-adjusted coed is a woman who plays a sport, has a crack professional internship possibility, steers a campus committee, volunteers to mentor a homeless child—and enjoys an avid sexual experience with the men who come her way. It's another "skill" she has acquired. That she would feel hurt or betrayed when a man moves on is a sign of weakness. This is the first cardinal rule: She is not supposed to *attach*.

I am sometimes asked, "Isn't it different among Christians?" Thankfully, it often is. Christians decry the hook-up scene—impersonal sexual liaisons for recreation, the lack of inhibition aided by copious quantities of alcohol. That the rest of our culture has made sex about as casual as "two airplanes refueling"[3] sometimes makes our sexual slipups appear less grievous by comparison. Christians, however, have a disturbing ability to compartmentalize our sexual lives from all that we know and believe about God, as though we've been left to construct our own sexual ethic.

Christian couples do insist on more commitment between them, but they are as tempted as anyone to satisfy each other sexually by every manner short of actual intercourse. They feel more guilt, though, as they sense that sleeping together or oral sex or mutual masturbation cheapens all they hold dear.

The relationship scene on the far side of college has changed for everyone. Gone are the days when weddings followed close on the heels of graduation ceremonies. Marriage is being deferred en masse. Instead, a woman in the prime of her twenties, at the height of her sexual power, enjoys a seemingly endless supply of attention from single men. The less-told reality, however, is that men get scarcer in a woman's thirties. About the time she is really ready to settle down—when her biological beeper starts to go off—she begins to ask, "Where are the men?" Like trains rolling into the station of her life, a good one comes by less often. Men have the unfair advantage of always having an accessible supply of younger women to choose from.

Out of the Ashes . . . Hope

When I hear the stories that emerge from the sexual lives of women now and I sense the lack of self-respect, the blow to their dignity, the choices in men made out of a fog of pain and loss, a deep note of grief strikes within me. I find myself wanting to protest, "You are meant to be loved and valued and cherished for the rest of your life by a man whose face lights up when he sees you." Whether a woman marries or not, strength and respect are her God-given birthright. I long to help women find the door back out of promiscuity and to recover the parts of their hearts and souls they feel they have lost. Doing so is entirely possible.

Considering what it has meant to grow up in a sexually charged culture with many of the natural barriers torn down, what kind of longings are stirred as you think about where you are in your relationships with men and where you would like to be? Those longings are more important than most of us realize. The desire for romance and the beauty of a good relationship, for deep connections with people that last through thick and thin, is like a homing device that God installs in our hearts early on; and unless we have completely short-circuited, this is the very desire that will lead us home, in the most real sense of the word.

Some say that today's young women have given in to "pre-emptive despair." They think that caring too much and hoping too hard just sets you up for disappointment, so why bother? But I believe there is a world of untapped desire in women who have been trained to shrug off their feelings and cop an image of bored detachment. Some things just don't change. As the Roman poet Horace said, "You may drive out nature with a pitchfork, yet she will still hurry back."

The longings of a woman's heart will not stay beaten down into an androgynous mush to satisfy a slanted view of human nature. "The desire to be pursued and courted, to have sex with someone you love as opposed to just barely know, to be certain of a man's affection and loyalty—these are deep female cravings that did not vanish with the sexual revolution," writes Washington journalist Danielle Crittenden in her exposé of modern women's lives.[4] Indeed, when you get down to brass tacks, most women long for one lasting love during their lifetimes. The reparation of broken relationships gets old before long, the glamour of male attention fades, and a woman starts to put her deeper longings into words:

> *Most women long for one lasting love during their lifetimes.*

"I want a man to want me for me, and I want the security of knowing that we intend to build a life together."

Even if a woman remains single, if she never marries, she must wrestle with the integrity of her own heart. Can she dole out little pieces of her self sexually and emerge as a whole woman with her self intact? What will she have in return other than perhaps a few good memories sprinkled throughout her mental scrapbook? Life in this sexualized society will not allow us to avoid the hard questions for long.

Our hair may be white and our face lined with wrinkles or we may be as young and fresh as Jennifer Aniston, with no makeup and hair tossed by last night's pillow, but in the places in us that matter most, age really makes no difference. Women are primed for the kind of deep and lasting attachment that so marks our lives—as someone's daughter, mother, aunt, sister, friend, or lover. An exciting career is just that—exciting. Excelling in a new sport is always a thrill. But what does any of it mean in the long run? Our lives are empty without relationships with those we love.

Fundamentally, it is this life of relationship that the sexual insanity of our day so threatens. Relationships, especially those between men and women, are inherently hard to sustain. They require every part of you—mind and body and soul—intact and capable of committing *your heart* into the safekeeping of another.

I invite you to explore the world of your sexuality in ways that perhaps you never have—to consider the power and beauty God pours out on you as a woman. Your sexual experience with men may be as pure as the driven snow. Or you may have known enough shame and heartache to fill a book. The good news is that beneath the ashes of all our pasts lies a golden core—the intrinsic, transcendent reality of being created in the very image of God as a woman. We cannot re-create our grandmother's day—and we need not. But if we listen to the longings of the heart God gave us, we will find our way home.

——— *Sexuality and Your Soul* ———

1. When do you feel not just the opportunity but the pressure to be sexual with a man? How do you feel about this?

2. What would more romance in a relationship look like from your perspective?

3. When do you encounter a sense of "preemptive despair," the notion that hoping for much of anything in a relationship is just a setup for disappointment? What effect does the refusal to hope have on relationships? On life as a whole?

4. If a woman remains single, yet moves from one sexual relationship to another, what will be the impact on her?

5. In terms of a "deep and lasting attachment" to a man, what qualities are you looking for in him? In the relationship itself?

Chapter 2

What Women Lose

That women may actually be the losers in the sexual revolution is an idea just dawning on this generation of young women, who feel as sexually free as it is possible to feel and yet are so often powerless to experience anything more with the opposite sex than unsatisfying, loveless flings.

Danielle Crittenden

The woman I am listening to slides back on the sofa, adjusting her skirt as though preparing for an important interview. Claire is a lovely woman about thirty years old, married to a man she met a couple of years ago in the law firm where she works. She is not too happy about being in a counselor's office, but she has to talk to somebody. There is tension in her marriage, and she's scared.

I ask her to tell me about the problem, which, of course, could be any number of things.

"Well," she starts in slowly, "it's sex. The problem is that I hate sex."

Occasionally I talk to a woman who is just plain honest—no fuss, no hedging, no effort to clean up a dirty elephant. *"I hate sex."* I hear this statement often these days.

Claire goes on to describe why she finds this part of her life so disagreeable. It's boring, she's been there before, she feels a trifle used—though she's not sure where this feeling comes from. She and her husband became Christians a few years ago, and she hoped this would change her feelings about sex, but it hasn't. "I could live my whole life and never miss sex." She almost whispers the words. She feels so guilty. After all, she's only thirty. Her husband is tired, not of sex but of her disinterest. He hints that he can't live like this—not feeling wanted sexually by his wife. Claire is beginning to panic.

Somewhere in this conversation, Claire starts to turn the pages of her life back ten years. She begins to talk about the first time she had sex.

"I didn't want to have a bad experience in losing my virginity—like some of my friends," she says. "So I found a guy I didn't feel anything special for, and I had sex with him. That way I could just get it over with."

"Losing your virginity was something you wanted to 'just get over'?" I think I must have heard Claire wrong.

"Well, sure. That way I wouldn't get hurt, or so I thought. Then maybe I would enjoy sex with guys I really cared about."

Somehow things didn't go according to plan. Sex became something Claire did to keep a relationship with a guy. Over the years, there were a lot of guys, including the man she eventually married. She loves him, but sex is stuck in the place it began for her. She knows it should be different, now that she is married.

"On my honeymoon, I could feel the jail bars coming down," Claire confesses. She saw herself facing a lifetime of feeling reluctant and used. She just hadn't expected that it would affect the overall health of her marriage this much.

⟵―――――――⟶

Sometimes, it takes awhile for women to feel the impact of sexual relationships with men they have known. After all, we live in a culture determined to minimize this impact and to treat sex as one more pleasure to be had between a man and a woman.

The emotional aftermath is usually swept under the rug, where it refuses to stay.

The truth is often much closer to Claire's story. Sex should be profound and not something associated with feelings of being used rather than of joy and sweet abandonment. But for many women, their experiences of physical intimacy have taken a toll.

Women feel the effect of broken sexual bonds more deeply than they like to admit. As the old expression goes, it takes two to tango, but sex that is not for keeps is generally harder on women. When couples break up, men seem to dust off their shoes and move on more easily than do women. Maybe they are just better pretenders, who knows?

For many reasons, women seem to pay a stiffer price. The pattern seems set even in the physical dimension, where the cold facts point to a woman's vulnerability. She is far more likely to contract a sexually transmitted disease than is the man with whom she sleeps. The most prevalent viral STD, for example, is human papillomavirus (HPV), a major cause of cervical cancer in women. Sexually transmitted diseases in women often operate like a stealth bomber, remaining silent and invisible for years. The symptoms are internal and hidden, where they are harder to detect, surfacing years later. Physical disease is an apt metaphor for what happens in the realm of the heart, in which the damage is real but often revealed only over time.

Sex that is not for keeps is generally harder on women.

Our basic orientation to life makes us more susceptible to the pain of sexual bonds that are made and then lost. Women are wired for connection. We could trace the cause all the way back to the Garden of Eden—to Eve, whose name means "mother of the living." Something about a woman's identity is anchored in the particular, rather wonderful ability to give life. She has the power to forge bonds, to create connections between people that outlast her own life and that literally give life to generations that follow her.

I wouldn't by any means limit this longing to connect to having children. In almost any setting, a woman will pick up important people clues, a seemingly innate form of emotional intelligence recognized only recently. Throughout our lives, single or married, in an office or at home, women are usually the ones who make relationships happen.[5] Women also feel more acutely the pain of relationships that fall apart. Recent neurological studies on men and women's brains show that when a woman feels an emotion like sadness, it affects six times more area of her brain than would be affected in a man's brain. The common expression that a woman "feels more deeply" has an actual physiological basis.

A woman is designed to forge a connection with a man that has the capacity for ever-increasing levels of depth and intimacy. She is inclined to build a lasting relationship with a man—one that can withstand the rigors of job changes, mother-in-law irritations, and the onslaught of wrinkles and root canals. Everything in her cries out for a relationship that endures. She is much less able to love a man and then leave him. For that macabre feat, she must be taught. The message that she should be able to walk off unaffected, as a man supposedly would, must be drilled into her. It does not come naturally.

Emotional Scarring

Ask any honest therapist who listens to people talk about their lives, and he or she will tell you how long and arduous the work of helping a woman through a painful breakup with a man can be. As one social commentator noted recently, "Getting over a relationship takes twice the time of the relationship itself. Women describe their post-breakup period like a flu bug that is hard to shake."[6] Journalist Danielle Crittenden explains the phenomenon:

> All the sexual bravado a girl may possess evaporates the first time a boy she truly cares for makes it clear that he has no further use for her after his own body has been satisfied. No amount of feminist posturing, no amount of reassurances that she doesn't need a guy like that anyway, can protect her from the pain and humiliation of those awful moments after he's gone, when she's alone and feeling not sexually empowered but discarded.[7]

Again, men don't escape the pain, but you won't see many of them agonizing in introspection, searching for their hidden flaws that must have surely, somehow, brought this breakup about.

I have found that women tend to ask more often the painful question, "What's wrong with me?" Physical intimacy feels like an investment of one's self. Thus, leaving or being left prompts a good deal of self-doubt and second-guessing. One's naked self feels exposed and unwanted. For many women, it is hard to pull out of this downward, introspective spiral. Even when a woman regains her objectivity, she still feels that it is a huge issue to risk another relationship. She asks, "How much of my heart am

I willing to trust a man with?" She measures out tiny bits of herself, reluctantly, never letting anyone get too close. Often she uses alcohol to dull her sensitivity and give her some sense of feeling safe and in control.

From this impossible bind, a woman often moves into a relationship she later regrets. She thinks, *I will find a man who appreciates me.* She chooses a safe man, but one hardly worthy of her affection. *I will find a man who won't leave me.* She accepts the attention of a man, ignoring glaring, red warning signals: He's thoughtless, inconsiderate, too often looking out for his own interests. But he's not going to leave. The pain of prying a woman apart from a man with whom she has bonded sexually can be wrenching—and blinding for some time to come.

One of the more hidden repercussions of combining sex and relationships is the way a woman can learn to step out of her body. It's a fairly easy maneuver. You just send your body out to relate to a man, but the real you floats in space somewhere essentially unconnected. Your body may experience pleasure, but you have stepped out of the moment. When things fall apart, you aren't affected as deeply—or so it seems. Sadly, this is nearly the exact same dynamic by which a woman can stay in an abusive relationship for a long time. Pretending rises to the level of an art form. She gets so used to stepping out of her body that she doesn't attend to the way she's being treated. As in Claire's story, it's an emotional "skill" learned in multiple sexual encounters.

Women often find that dabbling in the promiscuous locks many wonderful things about sex into the realm of the illicit. They find on the far side of marriage that the excitement and playfulness meant to accompany legitimate sex seem strangely off limits.

The struggle to decontaminate the legitimate, to reclaim what they know is meant for their good, can be enormous.

Loss of the True Feminine

One of the most confounding movements these days is our culture's push to convince women to deny their femaleness. A woman isn't supposed to feel anything. Not fear that her current relationship may not last. Not grief when it's over. Not a bit of tacky resentment when another woman comes into the picture. To feel something—to be hurt, betrayed, devastated—would be to admit that she had hopes and expectations at the outset. This is a big taboo. What would ever give her the idea that sex meant something or that her sexual favors were all that valuable? She should be able to walk away and expect nothing. The proof of our equality with men has become our ability to flat-line a broken heart.

Women often find that dabbling in the promiscuous locks many wonderful things about sex into the realm of the illicit.

There is something tragic about women not being allowed to express the loss and betrayal they feel when a relationship is over. Wendy Shalit turns her guns on this insistence that a woman not feel anything about broken sexual relationships.

> All those bad feelings we are too enlightened to feel nowadays—such as resentment, jealousy, betrayal— also signify the capacity to lose yourself in the first place, to fall in love with someone other than yourself. They presuppose that there is a soul to protect, that there are hopes to be shattered, a lost love to guard,

even if now only mentally and futilely. No hard feelings? I'm advocating a return to precisely that: hard feelings. At least then you know you're a person, that you have a heart.[8]

Oddly enough, as Shalit observes, it is the pain we feel when sexual bonds are made and broken that reminds us we were made for more. God made women to experience the joy of a lasting, enduring relationship with a man. That we cannot deaden our heart successfully is the best apologetic I know for the truth of how God made us.

Unfortunately, most of us turn these potent feelings back on ourselves. We think, *I need to be less sensitive. If I could only keep my heart from getting involved. There must be something wrong with me.* In a culture that trivializes everything transcendent, a woman's passionate nature is a bit embarrassing and, well, somehow bad.

Shalit calls this a new kind of misogyny—an effort to cure womanhood as though it were a disease. We can handle a woman starving herself into a size 4. A woman who demands the pay raise she's due is tough as nails. We can deal with her. But a real, living woman with hopes and dreams, with an unveiled longing for a good man and a child to tuck in at night—what does our culture say to her?

She needs to get some tear-proof mascara and a good antidepressant.

Perhaps we need to consider whether our culture's insistence that women treat sex as nonchalantly as men have tended to do is just a new face on the age-old devaluing of women and a woman's unique experience of life. As such, it does us little good to break through glass ceilings if a sexual lobotomy is the prize we win. A woman's orientation to the sexual experience—her intuitive sense that this is one aspect of a larger and lasting attachment—is not something she can shed like an old skin. Wendy Shalit goes on to make this observation:

> Maybe it is normal for a young woman to be "intense" and being cavalier is what is strange. Maybe wanting to forge bonds with others is normal, and it's cutting ourselves off from enduring attachments that is perverse. Maybe *not* having "rejection sensitivity" is what is sick, and *in*vulnerability to loss the real pathology. If being blasé about sex were natural, why would so many women have to be on Prozac in order to carry out what their culture expects of them?[9]

The Dehumanizing of Women

In this strange twilight zone of relationships, there is indeed a subtle paradigm shift taking place in the way our culture sees women. Perhaps the most brazen form of marketing sex as a product is the cultural icon Madonna. She trades on her sexuality—and in all apparent ways, successfully so. Madonna can hold an audience of eighty thousand people in the palm of her hand. Yet one of her former lovers claims that, privately, she is the most insecure woman he has ever known. "She remains at heart the little girl continually trying to win over her father, searching for love and acceptance," he says.[10] Madonna admits her in-your-face sensuality is a rebellion against her father, the Catholic church, and the world in general. Her life is an example of what happens to any woman when her sexuality becomes a means to an end. She may gain something momentarily only to discover the real stuff she longs for—love and acceptance—remains even more elusive.

My own awareness of the dehumanizing of sex came in the form of a high school senior getting ready to head for college. Her parents sent her to me, concerned that her grades were dropping, her interests flagging in everything save one new excitement—sex with her boyfriend. She could see no end in sight to this relationship. And nothing, she felt, compared with the warmth of his arms around her. Although she had been raised in a Christian setting, she absolutely did not see anything wrong with this arrangement.

"You know," she said, trying to enlighten me, "sex is just not what it used to be."

Sex is not what it used to be? I kept trying this comment on for size, wanting to understand where she was coming from. How could sex have changed? Slowly, I began to see her statement as a true expression for the way sex has been reduced to a tangible asset, a staple and a ware to be exchanged for the slim threads of love and attention. "I'll take what I can get now," she was saying. "Who knows what tomorrow may bring?"

Bear with me for a moment as I revisit a female institution that has been around longer than all of us put together. It's known as prostitution. In ages past, prostitution was a viable way (albeit a very sad one) by which a destitute woman with no visible means of support could provide for herself and her children. But at times using one's body for a material purpose has been given status and social acceptance. In nineteenth-century France, for instance, a whole culture of "courtesans" emerged. A woman could escape a drab existence and become a mistress with social standing for a prince or an archbishop—rich, important men who could provide her with a good living.

One story may provide a bit of a window here. Marie-Ernestine Antigony was just such a woman. At one point, her departure from Paris caused a traffic jam due to the thirty-seven coaches required to carry her beautiful clothing, jewels, and hats (the gifts of grateful men). Trouble came in the form of a poor tenor with whom she fell in actual love—dismissing her rich benefactors. Unfortunately, the tenor died two years later, and Marie lived out her last days at the mercy of other courtesan friends who provided for her until her death at the young age of thirty-four.

The parallels are worth considering. Neither a prostitute nor a mistress can expect anything of permanence—any real attachment to the man she is with. Both her body and her ability to charm is severed from the whole of who she is, offered as parts in exchange for something she needs or holds dear. The consequences are usually rather dire in the end: she is alone and spent, often ill, used up. *Alone.*

We have spent centuries trying to prevent women from being reduced to prostitution or beguiled into accepting the status of a mistress. We have come a long way. Now, indeed, we can pay our own bills. We have options, a future, a good education. So how in the world have we voluntarily agreed to return to the vestiges of the same paradigm? How have we let ourselves be reduced to trading sexual favors for something so ephemeral?

Reducing sex to a physical experience marks a slow drift back into the paganism from which Western culture was rescued. At one time, worship of the natural world reigned. The thinking was, What is more "natural" than the expression of sexuality, in whatever form it takes? There were no boundaries on sexual relationships and certainly no expectation that a man provide and care for a woman with whom he had a sexual relationship. Paganism then and paganism now has always led to the same place—the devaluing of women.[11]

The Need to Reclaim

A woman waits to talk with me after I have finished speaking in a seminar. She seems unusually patient, letting everyone else go in front of her, as though she is saving something for my ears alone.

She begins by telling me how her life recently has taken such a good turn. In her own words, she says she has found faith for the first time. She smiles when she tells me this. A relationship with God is something she ran from for many years but no more. Life is opening up on the inside of her, and she loves this. What she sees in this new light is how much she keeps people—men especially—at arm's length. Only so close and no closer. This troubles her.

She pours out her story. She lost her father when she was ten years old. They were in a car accident together, and she alone survived. She remembers the doctor and her mother coming to her hospital bedside to tell her that her father had died in surgery. She says she could feel a hole as big as her dad himself opening up inside her.

The first guy to pay her some attention was a junior in her geography class. She was a freshman. He had shoulders like two goal posts, and as he began to single her out, she felt better than she had for a long time. As spring moved into summer, she gave in to his persistent demand for sex. She didn't want to lose him or the feeling of specialness he gave her. But within weeks he had picked up with another girl. He moved through her friends like he was sampling a box of chocolates. A year or so later he admitted that her actual appeal to him had been her innocence. *Her innocence.*

"Where did you go from this relationship?" I asked her quietly. What I heard knotted up my insides. She had moved from this slap in the face to a string of guys, one after the other for the next seven years. "What difference does it make now?" she reasoned. Her hunger for a man to fill the void grew like kudzu in a swamp.

"Which of these guys treated you well? Have you known what it feels like to be really cared for by any man since your father died?" I asked, one question atop the other.

A little trail of tears slid down her cheek—a wordless, resounding no.

Many of us give away something precious before we know what we have. No one in our lives alerts us to our vulnerability; no one values our sexuality enough to struggle for its protection. Or perhaps we do not allow ourselves to hear one who wants to help.

Like Claire, at the beginning of this chapter, many of us found that early feelings of sexual pleasure that seemed mildly illicit intensified to potent feelings of fear of leaving or of being left. Now, though we are older and may be married, the thrill is gone. Perhaps, more accurately, the passion got diluted like a sexual dam that burst and spread water an inch deep over a wide field when it was meant to be a powerful river to nurture and sustain us for a lifetime.

For almost any woman who looks back over the debris of her sexual past, there is a measure of loss and regret. So much she wishes she could redo—or undo. The voice of one woman in her late twenties continues to haunt me. In wisdom beyond her years, she said, "I wish I hadn't given so much of myself. I feel that some of my experiences *thinned my soul,* and such an effect takes time to undo."[12] This thinning of the soul, of our capacity to enter into life and relationship with all we are, is perhaps the greatest loss of all.

I focus on the genuine sense of loss that goes with the territory of sexual bonds made and broken outside the parameters of marriage. For strangely enough, grief is what tells you that you were meant for more, that God made your body and your soul to be inextricably joined. Grief reminds you that you are human and that after all is said and done, you still have not managed—thank God—to amputate your heart. The first step to reclaiming anything of value is to be able to name the pain.

> *Grief is what tells you that you were meant for more, that God made your body and your soul to be inextricably joined.*

In this grief, we are not merely victims. No, our grief is the result of choices we have made. Perhaps, though, we are ready for someone to connect the emotional dots—to see our longing for an enduring relationship as something that is rightfully ours, something meant to be. The pain has meaning. Perhaps despite all the hype to the contrary, we actually long for someone to remind us of the beauty and passion and tender strength that is possible in a relationship with a man. A good man. Perhaps we are ready to let God do what only he can do, which is to restore us from the inside out.

Sexuality and Your Soul

1. Do you feel that women pay a stiffer price than men in the making and breaking of sexual bonds? Why or why not?

2. Where in this culture do you observe the insistence that you should be able to be sexually involved with a guy and not be emotionally attached?

3. What are some of the conclusions you have drawn out of the pain of a failed relationship? How do you see those conclusions now?

4. What parallels do you see between how women are asked to live in relationship with men now and prostitution? How do you feel about this?

5. When, in a relationship, do you feel used or sense you are in some way "using" someone else to meet your own needs?

Chapter 3

A Woman's Power

Women control not the economy of the marketplace but the economy of eros: the life force in our society and our lives. What happens in the inner realm of women finally shapes what happens on our social surfaces, determining [our] level of happiness, energy, creativity, and solidarity.

George Gilder

Like a solo rock star, [a male] must devise a bower, song, and dance that wows the gals. Among bowerbirds and most other animals as well, it's the females that do the choosing.

National Geographic, June 2003

$\mathcal{H}$e has driven all afternoon under a hot August sun just to surprise Sandy a day early. It took some real sweet talking to convince his boss he could make up the time later. But it will be worth the trouble, he's sure. His friends all complain. Why is he so scarce, so much less available to them? The days of fishing or playing golf all weekend are fading into memory. Since Sandy appeared on the landscape of his life, he's been strangely preoccupied. He used to vow he'd never do one of those long-distance relationships. Until he met Sandy. Now he's standing on her front porch with a grin as wide as Texas.

———

Sometimes it's amazing to what lengths a man will go when there is a particular woman he's set his heart on—in fact, the power of a woman in a man's life is a staple theme of many a good novel or movie. Just this week a big, tough policeman told me his own story about how one night he met an intriguing woman at a restaurant. They talked for hours, and after that he saw her every day for weeks. She had quite an effect on him. He stopped smoking pot, broke with his partying friends, and married her one year later. And he never looked back. "She's the best thing that ever happened to me," he confided.

This is a good example of the kind of power and influence a woman often has in a man's life. But power—specifically, the power of a woman—is not a topic you hear discussed much these days. Oh, we are well aware of the access to places of power that women now enjoy. Women fly bombing sorties and sit on professional boards and occupy choice seats in the best graduate programs—indeed, there is hardly a door left through which we may not enter. But in the intimate places of our lives, women are hesitant to claim a particular kind of power that belongs to us uniquely, the power that arises from our sexuality. It is not political in nature. It can't be acquired or copied successfully. It is so innate, so essentially female, that the best we can do with it is to realize it deeply and steward it wisely. And its glory is that it makes you different from a man.

The bad thing about a discussion of sexual power is that it implies something it is not—as though there are only winners and losers in the equation and your job is to make sure you emerge on top. True sexual power is a different thing. It rises out of the innate attractiveness God gave you as a woman, an allure that is incredibly desirable to a man. The attraction goes way beyond actual physical beauty. What a man is usually drawn to in a woman is two steps past her physical appearance. While he may lack words to express this, intuitively he knows he has stumbled on someone who can glimpse his heart, who seems to know him in ways he has always longed to be known. A man has

A man has a hunger that can only be touched by the innate kind of beauty you possess.

a hunger that can only be touched by the innate kind of beauty you possess.

Sexual power of this nature is really *creative power*—power that adds to both individuals and subtracts from neither. It leads to that wonder of wonders, the birth of new individuals and the establishment of a home that can span generations. It creates something infinitely valuable for all concerned—a true win-win situation. And therein lies the hint of tragedy. The other side of the coin is that when women squander their sexual power by doling themselves out piece by piece with nothing true and lasting required in return, everyone loses. Most of all, women lose.

In the intimate discussions that being a marriage and family counselor offers me, I often have opportunities to see the influence and power of a woman up close. I catch a glimpse in the devastated look on a man's face when the woman he loves says she will not try again to make their relationship work. I hear a man admit his fear. No matter how hard he tries, he may not be enough of *something* this woman needs, and perhaps, just perhaps, she will prefer another man to him.

I watch the ease of an elderly couple sharing coffee at McDonald's, the utter at-homeness they exude, the tender way he reaches for her hand to help her cross the parking lot. I walk past a good friend's desk at work, the space crowded by family pictures—his wife and children at the beach, his son playing football, his wife on their twenty-fifth anniversary. And suddenly I realize what he is saying without words: "This is the reason I show up day after grinding day."

I could point to all kinds of everyday things to illustrate the power of a woman. One story from the annals of World War II captures it well, and while the story itself may predate you, it offers a window into this mysterious and beautiful essence found in a woman. The event took place on D-Day as thousands of British, Canadian, and American troops stormed the beaches of Normandy under the rain of German gunfire. Wounded and dead men lay everywhere—the sacrificial offering that allowed other brave souls to scale the cliffs and slowly retake France piece by bloody piece. Under the rules of war, medics with bright red armbands were allowed to comfort the dying and care for the wounded.

Against all odds, there was a young French girl on the beaches of Normandy that day.[13] She ended up in the aftermath of the fighting quite by accident. Jacqueline Noel had ridden her bicycle to the beach hoping to retrieve a bathing suit her twin sister (killed two weeks before) had given her. She was wearing a Red Cross armband to permit her passage. When Jacqueline saw what was happening there on the beach, she stayed. She changed bandages, helped to haul the wounded out of the water, and did what she could to make herself useful. She stayed—for two whole days and nights.

For many years afterward when the men who survived the invasion of Normandy gathered at reunions, they debated whether there had actually been a woman on the beach with them that day. Perhaps it had been an angel, or maybe they had been hallucinating. Others assured them that indeed their memory was correct. Jacqueline herself actually married a British soldier she met four days after D-Day. They live today in a small French village near the coast.

Jacqueline says that over the years grateful veterans have shown up unexpectedly at her door seeking to speak with and offer thanks to the woman they remember as though she had appeared in a dream. Hundreds of male medics on the beach that day risked their lives again and again, yet no one seems to dream about them. There are no reports of streams of men seeking them out years later to discover their identity. *What is it about the touch of a woman in a moment of trauma and pathos that registers so deeply—indeed, that seems like a visit from an angel?*

The story of World War II itself is the picture of men who survived the war and then came home and married in droves (so much so, that by 1951 a baby was being born every seven seconds). Over and over in interviews these men admit that coming home to the arms of the woman they loved and seeing their children in their own backyard at play and at peace made the hardship of war worth the price. To come home was, quite literally, the reason they fought. It was not by happenstance that the nose of nearly every B-52 bomber bore the image of a woman.

Whatever this power of a woman is, it surely must be strong stuff.

What Is This Beauty About?

A woman's sexual power is closely tied to her innate beauty, yet there is no concept in our culture these days more conflicted than that of female beauty. Right away I must make clear that I'm writing about something deeper, more intrinsic, than a lovely face or body. The kind of beauty a confident woman possesses is an odd mix of mystery and warm allure that invites you always a little deeper into the essence of really knowing her.

Poets wax eloquent about this feminine essence. It's what a man hungers for—even when he thinks it's sex that he's after. The lyrics to Bruce Springsteen's hit song "Secret Garden" hint at this reality. He sings about the way a woman will let you into her heart, to remote parts of herself—if you are willing to pay the price. She will let you deep inside her, "but there's a secret garden she hides." A woman who knows her beauty understands that she has something incredibly valuable to give and something important to protect.

Unfortunately, beauty has received a good deal of bad press in the last thirty years. We have become slightly schizophrenic on the subject. Though we throw away our makeup and insist that the world take us "as is," huge numbers of us also find new and improved ways of achieving a beauty defined by thinness, starving our bodies until they comply—all in the pursuit of something we insist doesn't matter. It's a little like the days when Gloria Steinem, the feminist who swore that a woman needed a man like a fish needs a bicycle, could, nonetheless, be found hiding behind a magazine in New York's most elite salon getting her hair streaked so that she would be a tad more attractive for the good-looking men she was seeing at the time.

> *A woman who knows her beauty understands that she has something incredibly valuable to give and something important to protect.*

We keep this "schizophrenia" in place, I believe, because the longing to realize our beauty and to have this beauty known awakens something deep within us. And if we listen to this, we will become aware of an even deeper longing. We long for a man to see the worth in us and to cherish it—so much so that he returns over and over, always wanting more. It's scary to realize how deeply we long for something we can't guarantee.

One of William Yeats's most-loved poems, "When You Are Old," hints at what it looks like when a man has been able to let a woman's desirability guide him to the essence beyond the initial attraction. The voice is that of a man as he speaks to a woman he has known well for many years.

> When you are old and grey and full of sleep
> And nodding by the fire, take down this book,
> And slowly read, and dream of the soft look
> Your eyes had once, and of their shadows deep.
>
> How many loved your moments of glad grace,
> And loved your beauty with love false or true,
> But one man loved the pilgrim soul in you,
> And loved the sorrows of your changing face.

Is there a woman alive who does not long for a man who knows her so intimately that he sees and loves the "pilgrim soul" in her? It is so right to long for this, for this longing guides you to the best a man has to give. To know a woman's beauty to its depth is what a man was meant to desire deeply. This "secret garden" may not be something he ever truly realizes, but it is so appealing that he will spend the rest of his life in pursuit of it.

This provides one small but telling clue why the sexual relationship between a man and a woman is described biblically by the verb "to know." To know a woman was to be sexually intimate with her. This intimacy led in a hundred directions, unfolding layer after layer of endless possibility between two people. Conversely, "to lie with" a woman was just simply to have sex outside the constraints of marriage, and as such, it was expressly condemned. It is as though God says a man can't just sample the beauty and go on and not pay a price.

It is as though God says a man can't just sample the beauty and go on and not pay a price.

It is important to realize that this tender, inviting feminine beauty does not originate with a woman herself. It owes its source to the heart of God, to his very image imprinted at the depth of her being in all its loveliness.

Have you thought much about what it means to be created, as a woman, in the image of God? You could spend the rest of your life exploring this reality and not get to the end of it. No greater validation of your soul—your very self—exists anywhere than the reality of having God's image imprinted in your being. You are because he is. When the Father, Son, and Holy Spirit, who exist in perfect unity without erasing their individual personalities, set out to make human beings, they made male and female to adequately express what God is like. "Then God said, 'Let *us* make people in *our image,* to be like ourselves.' . . . So God created people in his own image; God patterned them after himself; *male and female he created them.*"[14] The essence of gender—being created as a woman—is rooted in the Trinity itself. You understand, then, why Pope John Paul once remarked that the thing wrong with pornography is that it doesn't show enough of a woman—it doesn't reveal her as a woman made in the image of God.

Some charge that God devalues women—after all, Jesus chose twelve men to be his disciples, and the biblical record was written by men. But such charges miss the deeper truth of a God who so esteems the feminine that he incorporates it into his very being. There are places in Scripture where God compares himself to a mother who cannot forget her child—indeed, one name for God in the original Hebrew is the "many breasted" one.[15] Every member of the Trinity—Father, Son, and Holy Spirit—moves in compassion, gentle correction, and faithful presence, which are traits we commonly associate with the feminine. Rather than undervaluing the feminine, God hallows it.

The earliest picture of woman in the Genesis creation story hints of this unique feminine beauty. After God has brought light into darkness, after he has made everything from a giraffe to a whooping crane, God creates Adam—a man who bears his own image, distinct from all the animals around him. But God does not stop there. From Adam's side, God makes Eve. She is God's finishing touch, and all Adam can say is, "Wow." "Eve embodies the beauty and mystery and tender vulnerability of God," writes John Eldredge. And then he quotes poet William Blake: "The naked woman's body is a portion of eternity too great for the eye of man."[16]

Eve stands as the pinnacle of God's creation. Or as Mike Mason puts it in his classic book about the mystery of marriage:

> My wife's body is brighter and more fascinating than a flower, shier than any animal, and more breathtaking than a thousand sunsets. To me her body is the most awesome thing in creation. Trying to look at her, just trying to take in her wild, glorious beauty, so free and primal, so utterly unchanged since the beginning of time, I catch a small glimpse of what it means that men and women have been made in the image of God. If even the image is this dazzling, what must the Original be like?[17]

A Curious Power

From this intrinsic attractiveness then, comes the particular power that women possess. You can sense it in a variety of settings—in the way smart men around a boardroom table stop and listen to a woman's intuitive hunch or in the instinctual way men look to a woman to provide an emotional sense of home and quiet refuge. But this "power" takes a particular form when it comes to the romantic dance between a man and a woman. And if we miss the importance of our power here, we will never be able to use it wisely.

Simply put, it is the power of yes and no. The delicate dance between a man and a woman makes you the decision maker in whether or not—or when and how—a man's most urgent physical need will be met. You can name the stakes. And while it may not feel like much "power" to you, a man knows that other than resorting to rape, he is at your mercy. God rests enormous power in the heart of a woman. The most vulnerable aspect of a man's being requires your permission, your reception of him. God makes a woman the prize to be won—a prize that is meant to go to a man worthy of her. She becomes "the ultimate worldly arbiter of a man's worth."[18]

The most vulnerable aspect of a man's being requires your permission, your reception of him.

For most women, the power of female sexuality is something we can feel and sense, but it is not something we have really considered. We grasp, however, even less about the sexuality of men, particularly the vulnerability they face. Women are simply more sexually secure than men. Believe it or not, we really are.

"The prime fact of life is the sexual superiority of women," George Gilder wrote in one of the most telling books on men to date.[19] By this Gilder means that a woman's body gives her many profound, repeated clues to who she is, and to her worth as a woman. She can give birth and nurse children at her breast, an incredible feat of creativity and accomplishment. A man is limited to one sexual act—intercourse—and for this act, he must perform. While a woman may or may not be into the sexual experience, if a man does not perform, it's a "show stopper," as they say. "For men, the desire for sex is not simply a quest for pleasure. It is an indispensable test of identity."[20]

For a man, there is simply more riding on this precarious venture called sexual intimacy. And this is yet another factor that tilts power in the direction of a woman. Gilder writes:

> This difference between the sexes gives the woman the superior position in most sexual encounters. The man may push and posture, but the woman must decide. He is driven; she must set the terms and conditions, goals and destination of the journey. Her faculty of greater natural restraint and selectivity makes the woman the sexual judge and executive, finally appraising the offerings of men, favoring one and rejecting another, and telling them what they must do to be saved or chosen.[21]

The beauty, allure, and sexual power you hold as a woman are holy things. They can bless beyond your wildest dreams or, as the biblical writer of the ancient proverbs observed, destroy everything you hold dear.[22] The choice is up to you. *How will you use this power?* You can pull a man toward you, make him as compliant as a well-trained puppy, use your sexual favors to seduce him or to try to bind his heart to yours. This pretty well defines the sexual manipulation game as it is played outside marriage. Or you can choose a slightly more challenging course. Your inherent modesty—conservative chic, if you will—translates into sexual power that buys you time and courage to consider the man before you.

How will you use this power?

What is he really like? What are his intentions? What kind of future with you does he have in mind?

The sexual power, the mysterious beauty at a woman's disposal, is such strong stuff that God means for her to confine it to one arena—marriage—allowing it to be part of the glue that bonds two people together, body and soul, for a lifetime.

A Power Embraced

In 1990 the movie *Pretty Woman* captured the imaginations of women, nearly catapulting the movie to the status of a classic. Julia Roberts gained instant fame in this story of a small-town girl turned prostitute who falls in love with a man for whom she only meant to provide a paid service. It's the tale of a man who is transformed by love he never intended to feel.

One scene in particular struck a very deep chord and sent me and most of the other women in the theater in search of the nearest Kleenex. If you've seen the movie, you probably know which scene I'm talking about. Richard Gere has made Julia Roberts an offer that all logic would dictate she should accept. He will put her up in a classy condo and give her a running credit account to buy whatever she wants just so she will be there waiting for him when he comes to town. She will be his mistress.

But in the few weeks they've been together, Julia has changed. She has shed the self-image of a prostitute. Instead, she sees herself as a lovely woman, much more aware of what she has to offer a man. The "pretty woman" has realized her beauty. She tells Gere that when she was a little girl her mother used to lock her in the attic when she was bad. She would pretend she was a princess in a tower, and a knight would come charging up with his colors flying. She would wave, and he would climb the tower to rescue her. And then comes Julia's vintage line: "Never in all that time did the knight say, 'Honey, I'll put you up in a great condo.' A few months ago I would have taken your offer. Now everything is different. *I want more*" (emphasis mine).

I wonder how many of us long to say words just like that to a man. "No, I will not accept the crumbs under the table." How many of us are aware of wanting more—of longing for a man who sees in us a love he cannot do without? A man who does not insist on separating sex from marriage? How many of us long for the courage to just put it out there like Julia Roberts: *No. I want more.*

To claim your true sexual power is to embrace the courage and strength of that statement. It means you refuse to squander this power by doling yourself out in bits and pieces in the relationship of the moment. Sexual power is right at the heart of who you are as a woman. It is power that is rightfully yours. When sex is an investment you make in the love of your life, it multiplies into a storehouse of pleasure and intimacy that blesses every other part of your life with a man. That's what it was meant to be—a rich joy stored up for you by the mercy of God.

This kind of power belongs to you innately. It is your birthright. And yet, oddly enough, you will only be able to experience its importance in a relationship when you have first deeply embraced it for yourself.

Sexuality and Your Soul

1. What are some of the negative and positive connotations for you regarding the idea that you, as a woman, have an innate sexual power given to you by God?

2. When do you catch a glimpse of this power?

3. When Bruce Springsteen wrote about a woman's "secret garden," he was describing the deep essence of a woman that is so inviting to a man. How would you describe the "secret garden" in your own heart? What do you want a man to take the time to get to know about you?

4. What evidence do you find for the value that God places on the feminine—on the essence of being created a woman, not a man? What draws you about this? What scares you?

5. That God allows a man's sexual vulnerability to be subject to your permission, your reception of him, is a huge thing. What do you hear in this? How does it motivate you?

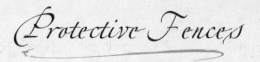

Chapter 4

Protective Fences

Our mothers pined for liberation, and we are pining for interference.

Wendy Shalit

People always say, "She's such a pretty girl—she must have loads of boyfriends." Sometimes I think I sleep with men to prove that I'm attractive—I'm normal. I have sex so people won't think there's something wrong with me.

Amy, age 22

*I*n that great citadel of American culture, the shopping mall, we are accosted by images that startle us with their glaring sensuality. Like everyone else, I mill through the crowd in search of some frivolous item. Out of nowhere, a larger-than-life billboard stops me dead in my tracks. A beautiful couple has been caught by a camera lens in a very private moment, halfway to naked. They are busy disrobing each other of the very clothes being sold inside this store. The picture nearly pulsates with heat. Does anyone else see this? I cannot help but look around—it's almost an involuntary motion. Surely other people in the mall are searching out the store manager to ask how he or she can bear to market jeans this way. Surely. *How do we permit this?* I find myself wondering. *Can anything sold by this means be worth the human cost?*

Once again I feel raw, cold air blowing through the door of restraint, a door my generation knocked clear off its hinges. And I shudder, I am appalled at the lack of protective boundaries around sexuality these days. I knowing it hasn't always been like this—this "wordless tossing of our girls to the wind,"[23] with so little effort to protect and shelter.

Parents, of course, have always formed the first wall of protection. Their job seems to get more difficult all the time. Many struggle with the budding sexuality of their offspring who confront the rigors of hormones. Parents wonder what to do in the face of all the pressure for their children to be sexual. Should they encourage a daughter to get on birth control just in case? Should they tow a hard line—or give in and simply insist (as some parents do) that when kids use their home for a party they bring their own clean sheets?

When you think about the voices in your past, who were the people who went out of their way to talk about sexuality with you? Talking about sex with a daughter can make for a rather awkward conversation, but if there is little or no dialogue at all, it can leave a girl feeling as though she's on her own. A parent may think, *Maybe the stakes aren't that high. Maybe she can just drift in the direction of what comes naturally and nothing much will happen.*

Yet parents have always been only part of the picture. These days we seem to have lost our collective will as a culture to nurture and protect the sexuality of kids. The results of our lack of protective boundaries blows into offices like mine with great regularity. It arrives in the shape of a young woman, usually a year or so out of college and into the first good job that provides her space to assess her life. She is just old enough to have gained some perspective and can see life more clearly. And what she sees in this new light are little shreds of her self that need to be stitched back together by a good seamstress.

She comes wondering why she feels hollow, empty, and unable to take much risk in any close friendship. All these guys line up in her head—the ones she loved, the total jerks, the ones whose names she can't remember. She knows she can't turn clingy in relationships now because that's a big turnoff. But

> *"Why didn't I hear more about the cost of living as if sex has no consequences, no meaning?"*

what can she do when she's lost her bearings, feels so alone, and wonders where God is in all this? One woman I talked with asked, "Why didn't I hear more about the cost of living as if sex has no consequences, no meaning? *Where was everybody?*"

Of Wedding Veils and a Father's Permission

The cultural walls placed around issues of sexuality for a long time and for good reason have eroded. Every generation until now has fashioned means by which a man and a woman could get to know each other without sexual attraction taking over the relationship. For this reason, front parlors came in handy. A couple could be alone—but not too alone. Front porch swings were the rocking incubator of many an emerging romance. The primary force to contend with, at least historically, was one's father or, if he was absent, one's brother. Of all things expected of a man, protecting the innocence and purity of a daughter or a wife or a sister was right at the top of the instinctual list. As in the movie *Braveheart,* William Wallace could not ride up to his love's Scottish hut and whisk her away for a few hours without first encountering a large and hairy obstacle—her father.

The kinds of practices that protected women have a long and colorful history. Ancient Jewish law, for example, corralled the sexual experience to the bonds of marriage between one man and one woman for a lifetime, and then it celebrated the place of sex. For example, the government could not conscript a man for war during his first year of marriage, because bringing pleasure to his wife was literally his job description: "If a man has recently married, he must not be sent to war or have any other duty laid on him. For one year he is to be free to stay at home and bring happiness to the wife he has married."[24] And the biblical Song of Songs is perhaps the most joyful celebration of sex in ancient literature.

What is the message you hear in these boundaries that were kept in place for ages? They may sound like a bunch of clever devices invented by uptight people to stifle the pleasure of kids who have too many ideas and too active hormones. But the picture is bigger than this. What these boundaries most essentially convey to a woman is *value*. As the ancient Jewish saying goes, "The daughters of Israel are not available for public use." Their lack of sexual availability stems from their high value. Putting a fence around sexual expression is a way of saying you are special. Your innocence and purity belong to you alone. They are part of the giving of yourself to a man—an incredible gift. A healthy society will protect your sexual innocence, not exploit it in the rush for a bigger profit margin.

Even the book of Proverbs (the one book of the Bible famous for being utterly practical) includes a verse that says, "Do not move an ancient boundary stone set up by your forefathers."[25] The idea is that we need to be cautious when we think of dismissing a cultural boundary that has been recognized and heeded for generations. And this is what makes my own generation's dismissal of the worth of virginity so arrogant. Those before us were not stupid, and we are not smarter than they were.[26]

Promiscuity has increasingly devolved to mean sleeping with two men during the same period of time. In other words,

"I'm okay as long as I don't sleep with Harry when I'm actually seeing Jim." Even as Christians, we often pretend that the clear teaching of Scripture regarding sexuality must be adjusted for our enlightened experience of modern life. The Bible, though, speaks to who we are at our core, who we are created to be as a man or a woman. The desire to be known and loved and cherished never changes. And the personal effect of sex outside marriage does not lessen, no matter how hard I try to minimize the impact. It's bigger than I am and older than my time. To ignore the boundary simply means that I wreck my life crashing into it.

Even apart from historical precedent, have you ever thought about the relational function that sexual boundaries create in your relationships with men? A kind of exquisite tension develops as a romance takes off. You are forced, in all the best ways, to push out the borders of your relationship. You have a special span of time to stockpile the building materials of a relationship that can last—the sense of being enjoyed by another, respect, and especially trust. Without trust nothing lasting is built in a relationship. Allowing for a period of life devoted to courtship without sex is the best gift two people in love could claim for themselves. It is the heart of romance.

Without trust nothing lasting is built in a relationship.

But once sex enters the scene, it dominates the whole picture for a while—and rightly so. Sex was meant to be consuming. That's what honeymoons are for: giving couples some time for the celebration of sex. And that's why people with good memories leave a couple alone for a fair number of months after they are married.

Sex is God's idea, his good gift to married couples. The parameters drawn around the sexual experience are not the work of a killjoy. They are meant to enhance pleasure and freedom and to lead us to our deepest longing, which is ultimately to experience union with God himself. For this reason, Christians and Jews alike insist that sex is holy, that is, it is set apart and sacramental.

If you grew up with the notion that having boundaries around sex is an artificial restriction that will repress your natural personality, I encourage you to ponder this question, especially as you walk through a shopping mall: How many sectors of our society line their pockets on the commercializing of sex? Who is profiting from catapulting women into sexual expression and license that masquerade as freedom?

I guarantee it's not you or any women you know.

Feeling Tossed to the Wind

Of course, the sad irony in this situation is that women have clamored for total sexual freedom, the absence of sexual boundaries. So in a sense we are being burned by a fire we fanned, yet we seem surprised when we are burned. Slowly, often in retrospect, it is dawning on us that something vital is missing. We can catch a drift of it in the wind—a low, mournful longing for the protective fences that used to be in place.

The sad irony in this situation is that women have clamored for total sexual freedom, the absence of sexual boundaries.

Women often look back on losing their virginity and wish that more had been made of the significance of their innocence—as though it could only be *seen* in the rearview mirror after it had been lost. Thousands of girls can identify with Naomi Wolf, whose book *The Beauty Myth* exposed the way our culture's demand for "beauty" exploits women. Wolf writes about the day she and her high school boyfriend made an appointment at a local health clinic so she could be fitted for a diaphragm and they could have sex. "The young, bearded doctor who fitted me treated it all as if he were explaining to me a terrific new piece of equipment for some hearty activity such as camping or rock climbing," she writes. It was like a trip to the vet, like being processed on an animal level.

She goes on to make this observation:

> In terms of the mechanics of servicing teenage desire safely in a secular, mechanistic society, the experience was impeccable. The technology worked and was either cheap or free. But when we walked out, I still felt there was something important missing. It was weird to have these adults just hand over the keys to the kingdom, ask, "Any questions?," wave, and return to their paperwork. . . . It was easier than getting your learner's permit to drive a car.[27]

For Naomi Wolf, the experience of sex itself was a trifle disappointing—not awful, certainly not good. It was what it was. She remembers kissing her boyfriend good-bye and going home to think about what had happened—and getting angry. "That's it?" she said to herself. "That's all my virginity is worth?" In a secular culture, no moral context is ascribed to the experience of sex; it has the meaning you give it. But the tip-off that sex is far more than a physical act lies in the anger and disappointment and loss this woman felt.

In the Christian community, this story may seem a bit extreme. Hopefully this isn't your story—not even close. But it does describe well the culture you find yourself in, where the pressure to be sexual is everywhere. Where are the voices in your life that have validated your worth as a woman, your right to say no, your obligation to regard your virginity as something too valuable to be doled out for the moment? I hope with all my heart that these voices have been loud and credible in your ears.

In the absence of protective boundaries and a moral context for sex, many a woman develops her own ethos for what she considers promiscuous behavior. For instance, if you get drunk at a party, hook up with a guy, and end up having sex with him, you aren't truly promiscuous because you weren't fully aware of what was happening. If you make a conscious choice to have sex, then maybe someone would call you a slut, but "drawing a blank" absolves you of anything that resembles guilt. Witness, then, the rising use of alcohol on college campuses.

In a Culture That Lacks Moorings

In her book *Reviving Ophelia,* Mary Pipher writes about the effect on girls of growing up in a culture that no longer provides the protective boundaries it once did. She notes, as many have, the expansive sense of the world with which girls come into adolescence. Anything seems possible to them, and they are ready to explore all kinds of possibilities. This, she bemoans, comes to a halt as they enter adolescence and confront the sexualization of their gender. Suddenly they are asked to behave and appear as feminine in a culture where femininity is defined by nothing more than sex. Pipher calls this the way girls "crash and burn in a social and developmental Bermuda triangle."[28] In a sad, paradoxical way, the fact that women crash and burn without these protective boundaries around sexuality testifies to their transcendent nature—a boundary *is* intended to be in place.

Have you noticed the way boundaries that protect virginity and innocence serve, strangely enough, to bring women onto equal footing with men? Without those boundaries, our vulnerability is exposed and often exploited, and we become what we most hate—the weaker sex. We are left to march around with placards decrying the brutish treatment of men. Our feminine nature is exhibited, only more in victimization than in real strength.[29]

As a culture, we have surrendered our responsibility, intimidated by the feminist notion that it is sexist to protect girls. That a woman's experience of sex and love is different from a man's is a reality evident to anyone with open eyes, but this truth so rebukes our timidity regarding gender differences that, like the proverbial elephant in the living room, it cannot be named. We would rather surrender our girls than change our ideology. We are profoundly in need of some sort of "ism" that honors the real experience of women.

Longing for Limits

There is a growing cry, not necessarily for a return to the nostalgic past, but for some new form of boundaries that protect the sacredness of sex. Especially for women who long ago lost their virginity, there is a longing to regain the innocence of soul that boundaries imply. You can hear this cry in the words of a woman who felt pressured into sex by college roommates who were openly hostile to her desire to remain a virgin. They threatened to ostracize her, so she gave in to a boyfriend who shortly thereafter deserted her. Years later she looked back on the experience this way:

> Premarital sex creates self-hatred in women.... Perhaps I am overstating my case. However, I have been through a lot of pain—the years of trying to patch together the wreckage of my self-esteem, the loss of innocence, the desire to feel clean and whole just out of my reach. Although I have had a few marriage proposals, none of the men who proposed were appropriate, and I am still unmarried at 37. I feel that if I had been allowed to be a virgin, I would have had a much healthier approach to "courtship." ... *A healthier society would protect women from premarital sexual experience.*[30]

What do we do in the absence of a protective society? To what do we turn when there are no front parlors to be had? When we find ourselves finally ready for limits, where do we go to get them? These are the ultimate questions. We live in a culture so sexualized that the protective fences around sex must be inside one's own head. *The boundaries must be internalized.* As you read this book, you may be taking your own steps to establish or to reclaim an inner sense of sexual boundaries. Sometimes we don't even know we've crossed a boundary until we go back and see what we stumbled over.

There is a longing to regain the innocence of soul that boundaries imply.

This process is inherently spiritual in nature, meaning that the boundaries are real because they are rooted in something that transcends one's own individual life or culture. They are timeless, true in the deepest sense of the word—the laws of God's relational universe. I embrace them, then, precisely because they are larger than my own life. I fit my life within these sexual boundaries and find, as it were, my own front parlor in which to get to know a man.

When it comes to boundaries and limitations of any sort, the way we perceive them means everything. Do I see sexual boundaries as restrictive or freeing? Do they lead to a loss of life and pleasure, or are they the actual gateway to the thing I most want in terms of genuine relationship?

The frame we put around this inner picture is crucial. As a life principle, boundaries are meant to protect something so that it can be enjoyed in its true form. The rubric applies in a host of ways. Think of the taboo associated with incest in a family, for example. What makes incest so destructive is that, in the act of transgressing these boundaries, you lose a father or a brother, as such. The sexual boundaries God establishes are a window into his heart to protect for us the goodness of all that lies inside. As Jesus clearly said, "I have come that they may have *life*, and have it to the full."[31]

Laying claim to the sanctity of sex as that which is reserved for the love a man and woman share in the moral context of marriage is to reclaim the integrity of one's own soul as well. For women who lost their virginity somewhere along the way, it is like taking back ground lost in some misbegotten war. They see something rich and meaningful and entirely possible on the horizon—a relationship with a man that is unfettered and nourishing, without the sexual baggage of having slept together.

If there is anything good about living in a culture that sells sex by the yard, it's that sexual boundaries cannot easily be imposed from without. They have to be claimed—or reclaimed—from within, where the only real boundaries are formed. They are not being forced on you by parents or a college handbook or cultural norm.

Real boundaries are those you embrace for yourself.

Sexuality and Your Soul

1. If our mothers threw off restraints and today's women pine for "interference," as Wendy Shalit claims, in what ways do you see women wanting to be interfered with—wanting someone to encourage their sexual integrity?

2. What kind of protective fences have there been in your life regarding your sexuality? Whose voices have been preeminent?

3. How have you felt about these influences?

4. In the absence of sexual boundaries, how do you see women becoming "the weaker sex"? In what ways does this increase our vulnerability?

5. What would you need in order to internalize a sense of sexual boundaries so that they are not about deprivation but about freedom and choice?

Chapter 5

Stepping on Each Other's Toes

We all need a little tenderness. How can love survive in such a graceless age?

> From "The Heart of the Matter,"
> sung by Don Henley

Carelessly, thoughtlessly, casually, sex—in the short space of a single generation—went from being the culminating act of committed love to being a precondition, a tryout, for future involvement. If any.

> Danielle Crittenden

*E*very generation has had a version of this particular dance—the delicate, breathtakingly beautiful dance between a man and a woman. Whether you called it courting, dating, or just hanging out, there is no experience quite like falling in love. The secret longing of every woman's heart is to be wooed and won. This is the heart of romance.

Even in this age of ironic detachment, this longing shows up occasionally in full force. It sneaks out when we aren't looking. In recent years, I have begun to show a clip from the movie *Braveheart* whenever I speak on this subject. Something about Mel Gibson speaking in Scottish brogue seems to strip away time and modernity until the viewers are just simply men and women looking for the love of their lives and a cause that matters. Perhaps you will remember the story I am about to describe.

In an unforgettable scene, William Wallace comes calling for Murron, a young woman to whom he has been attracted for some time. The family banters back and forth until suddenly Murron leaps onto the back of William's horse and together they ride bareback across the vast glen. They spend the afternoon getting to know each other. He tells her all the places he has been, worlds away from Scotland, and speaks in French about how lovely he finds her. She is suitably wowed. The birth of this love closes with a scene of the two of them sitting atop a cliff watching the distant sunset. This is a love William is willing to risk everything for. And indeed, Murron's death at the hands of the king's soldiers is the catalyst that incites him to war against England for the freedom of Scotland.

When I show this film clip, it is almost always followed by complete silence—not a sound in the room. For a few moments, a deep, ageless place in each of us opens up. Our cynical aloofness is stripped away to expose the raw, aching longing for the kind of beauty that is possible only between a man and a woman.

We see this beauty captured on occasion at a wedding. Against a backdrop in which everyone present knows the couple will face their own measure of heartache and trouble ahead, each pledges love and commitment to the other in the face of the great unknown. The courage required, if you really think about it, is staggering. The beauty of the event is a borrowed one, on loan from the story of the ages that will end at a wedding and lavish feast. The Bridegroom awaits even now. The bride is making herself ready for the day when the Bridegroom has promised to present her to himself "without stain or wrinkle or any other blemish."[32]

There is a simple, timeless beauty to this courting dance itself: discovering someone you click with, having him go out of his way to be with you, feeling really at home together, and experiencing an odd, inconsolable ache when he is away. When the soil of your heart is primed to receive love, this courting dance is a clean and beautiful thing. Every generation recognizes this beauty and bows its head with wonder. Agur, one of the writers of Proverbs, commented on the dance:

> There are three things that are too amazing for me,
>   four that I do not understand:
> the way of an eagle in the sky,
>   the way of a snake on a rock,
> the way of a ship on the high seas,
>   *and the way of a man with a maiden.*[33]

Nothing compares with the beauty or the sheer, inscrutable mystery of a soaring eagle among the clouds or a ship on a bright blue sea—or a man and woman falling in love.

Being tuned for the beauty of relationship is what makes us also so acutely aware of the travesty when things turn cheap and ugly. For as much beauty as you can find in relationships, there is a similar amount of pain. There is surely nothing beautiful about a broken heart. This delicate, romantic dance can easily turn into a painful experience of stepping on each other's toes.

Who's on Top?

Promiscuity in a relationship affects the dance in a big way. It's like throwing a grenade on the coffee table—destruction and chaos enter the picture. Men as well as women feel the effects because their dance steps are literally altered. The question I would explore is, How does promiscuity jeopardize this fragile beauty in a relationship, such that it leaves men and women alike off balance, insecure, reeling to dissonant music?

When Masters and Johnson, the noted sexual researchers of the 1960s, set out to emancipate men and women from sexual constraints, they admitted that they had no idea where their experiment would lead. Now, after all these years, where have we come? What is happening in this brave new world of relationships with no holds barred? How does the expectation of sexual favors alter the dance between men and women?

> *How does the expectation of sexual favors alter the dance between men and women?*

When sex is introduced into a relationship outside of marriage, immediately the stakes are raised and the term "jealous lover" comes into play. The one who is penalized is the one whose heart is most involved, and the person on top is the one who actually cares least. He or she can walk away with the least angst. Sex throws the dance into a kind of power maelstrom, with each person vying for the place that feels safest.

A woman once came to talk with me about a man named Matt, an old boyfriend who kept hanging around. They had been each other's first sexual relationship, and they had been together for three years. Things had ended between them more than a year before, but Matt wouldn't go away. She was almost through college, and Matt continued to call and show up wanting to talk just as she was getting off work. What would have been, in the absence of a deep sexual connection, a much simpler parting became a painful breakup that bordered on stalking.

Injecting sex into a relationship that has no covenantal basis tends to turn sexual favors into a tool. Many a woman on the far side of marriage reluctantly admits that she used sex to gain commitment from a man. She even enjoyed the process. Sex was different back then—it was exciting and forbidden, and it had a purpose. It was something she used to gain a sense of control in the relationship. After marriage, though, the story takes a different turn. Sex still seems like a tool, only now she feels like the one being used. She has a whole mind-set to undo—all the shame and guilt she came to associate with sexual desire.

The beauty of the dance is jeopardized when you have to wonder if a man would be interested in you, just you, without a sexual relationship, when you feel like you have to give sex to get love, when there is no freedom to just get to know someone without pressure to be sexual.

Expecting Too Little from a Man

Another way in which the beauty of the dance is being lost is that allowing sex to be part of a dating relationship invites men to be their worst selves. Indeed, it is a common complaint among women—men seem to be more boorish, as though they have a right to expect sexual favors.

I remember the first time my car radio played Lou Bega's song "Mambo No. 5." In a catchy little tune, Bega sings about wanting "a little bit" of Sandra, and some of Mary and Jessica as well. In fact, the sampling of any woman sexually is enough to make him her man—at least for a while. I kept turning up the volume because I could not believe the audacity. I wanted to throw my coffee cup at the car radio! And yet I recognized in these lyrics the vastly lowered standards for men now and the kind of behavior we are accepting as vaguely normal.

How often these days does a guy pull out a chair for you or walk ahead to open the door before you get there? When is the last time a man asked you how you felt about something he said or did? How many men in your life would you think of as being really considerate, who go out of their way to do something for you just to be thoughtful? This used to be the bare minimum in a man you'd think twice about.

In the great androgynous experiment we have lived through, wherein it seems weak to expect a man to treat you differently because you are a woman, we have raised a generation of men who are trained to think that women are just like them. To give them special treatment would imply that they are needy in ways that men are not. We cannot be too surprised at men's boorish behavior. If sex is what they want from a relationship, they assume this is what a woman wants, too. "No" has historically been seen as a woman's rightful prerogative. But in today's sexual climate, "no" is interpreted by many men as a personal rebuke to something they thought they had a right to expect.

"Men *are* getting away with appalling behavior toward women. But we are letting them get away with it—and then . . . refusing to admit it to ourselves," writes social commentator Danielle Crittenden.[34] Allowing a relationship to turn sexual sends a signal that men read clearly: You don't have to be responsible. It tells a guy that very little is expected of him, and sure enough, he conforms to this expectation. It is no compliment to a man, however. He knows he is getting away with something. And part of him realizes that he does not deserve your respect, which in the male psyche is the validation he most truly craves.

> *Allowing a relationship to turn sexual sends a signal that men read clearly: You don't have to be responsible.*

Sexual license in a relationship tends to cancel out customary graces, as though telling the truth even when it's hard or other such selfless acts are small, unimportant courtesies. It makes the whole dance more about what I'm getting than what I'm giving, and this is the beginning of the end in any relationship. Promiscuity is, by definition, a "taking" event, a loud way of saying, "I will have my needs met," and as such, it paves the way for our worst character to emerge.

Have you noticed that in some crucial way a man wants you to expect the world from him? He sees in the mirror of your expectations someone who believes the best about him. And if you see him as a guy worthy of respect, able to look out for you and other people, someone who has his head together, then he believes it a little more of himself. You do him no favor when you expect too little. Wendy Shalit says, "Too many egalitarians equate male gentleness or protectiveness with subordination, while too many conservatives equate it with effeminacy. Both sides are wrong. A man should be gentle around a woman. That's part of what it means to be a man."[35]

Sex in a Relationship You Hope Is for Keeps

Always the question emerges, Isn't sex in a committed relationship a little less injurious? Even more, is it not totally understandable when it happens between a couple who have an "understanding" of sorts that marriage is in the offing? Is not the beauty of the relationship preserved?

This is a hard question to answer. If you compare it to building a house, it is like hoping the house can be built successfully even though something is chipping away at the foundation as you build. It can be done. Good houses are constructed under duress. But who would willingly want to take those risks with the central human relationship of their lives?

The major building block of a close and intimate relationship is trust. Marriage vows are the equivalent of looking someone straight in the eye and saying, "As much as I am able, I trust you above all others with my life." Sex before marriage eats away at this very trust. Always the nagging question hangs in the background: How would you feel about me if sex weren't in this picture? Do you love me for me?

Couples who have sex before marriage find that jealousy and mistrust creep in more easily on the far side of the honeymoon. They know a boundary has been crossed once. Since neither had the strength of will and character to prevent sexual intimacy between them, what's to keep from crossing a sexual boundary again, only this time with someone else?

Especially as it regards marriage, sex clouds the issue at hand. It's so hard to think straight! I hear many men and women admit after marriage that they did not really know the person they married—not really. Sex filled in the spaces. After a while they weren't sure if the attachment was sexual or to the person. It all got blurred. Combining sex with a serious relationship among two people not yet married is a bit like going drunk to an art auction where you intend to sink your life savings. If ever you needed to make a decision with your head, marriage is it. Who is this man? Is a future together wise?

Devaluing Yourself as a Woman

One rainy fall day a woman came to my office and told me how tired she was of the whole dating scene—if you could call it that. What she meant was that she had gone from one relationship to the next for the last six years, and she despaired of ever finding a guy she would want to bring home to her parents.

"I'm seeing a man right now who seems almost too good to be true," she said a little wistfully. "It's only been a couple of months, but I'm just waiting for him to stop calling or to pick up with someone else."

"Are you telling me that you see some red flag in this guy?" I asked, thinking maybe he wasn't as good as he looked.

"No," she said quickly. "It's not him. It's me. I'm waiting for him to find something about me he doesn't like. There must be something I'm missing."

I hear this kind of comment too often, and it always saddens me. Like this woman, it usually comes from the lips of someone who has had a parade of men through her life—a string of sexual relationships—and the hope she has given up is about herself. She no longer sees herself as a woman who has something wonderful to offer a man. Too many men have left. She can't expect that some man would truly want to woo and win her for the long haul rather than the moment. At the bottom of her soul sits a statement perilously close to this: "I don't deserve to be loved."

This is where the dance between men and women loses nearly all its beauty. It's not that there's something wrong with her; it just *seems* that way when too many guys have come and gone. After a while, though, this self-devaluation becomes a self-fulfilling prophecy. How you see yourself becomes the way you invite others to see you.

Truthfully, I know of no way out of this dark place in the forest other than turning to a love that is bigger and deeper than any man's—the cleansing, restoring love of Jesus Christ. You can try every self-help remedy available, but none of them get to the source of the pain—the shame of seeing yourself as less than lovable.

I often am drawn back to the gospel story of a woman who knew more shame and rejection than most of us will encounter in a lifetime.[36] Picture this scene with me. It is early morning; the sun is just beginning to warm the stones beneath bare feet. Jesus is preparing to teach in the temple court, but a loud commotion interrupts him. A woman, half naked, clothed in shame, is dragged before Jesus by a group of men who want to stone her to death, her lawful punishment. Her sin? Having been caught in the act of adultery. (One wonders where the man involved went.)

No one rises to the woman's defense. She makes no plea, no attempt to escape. She has no advocate. She is stripped of honor and any sense of worth. Those who have dragged her before Jesus are not really concerned about her adultery and certainly are not concerned about her. Their only goal is to trap Jesus. Will Jesus uphold the law that permits her stoning? How will he deal with a guilty woman?

Jesus does not answer her accusers at first. He stoops down and writes in the dirt something mysterious and unrecorded in the text. Then he issues a challenge that turns everything on its heels. "Let any one of you who is without sin be the first to throw a stone at her,"[37] he says, and one by one, beginning with the oldest, the men walk away until Jesus is alone with this woman.

She could run away easily now and hide in the shadows of her shame. But she chooses to stay with the one person who could justifiably cast a stone. She is in no hurry to leave. Perhaps this is the first time in her life she has felt entirely safe in a man's company. Jesus straightens up and looks into her eyes. This moment is just between the two of them.

"Woman, where are they? Has no one condemned you?"

"No one, sir," she said.

"Then neither do I condemn you. Go now and leave your life of sin."[38]

A close friend who for years has coached people through significant life change says that people never really change very deeply until someone catches them in their shame and is not appalled. That's exactly what happened in this gospel account. Jesus caught this woman in the place where everyone else would throw her away—the place of her sin and shame. But he takes her by the hand and leads her to freedom.

This story holds the secret to how any woman discovers the love of God in the places in her soul she would most want to hide. Jesus sees, as no one ever has, the broken, sinful places in our soul where we have sought every other love but his—where we feel like a prostitute, where we think of ourselves as undeserving of love, where we know that no one who saw us this way would want us.

Jesus does not turn away. He steps right into the mess we have made and offers us not another stone of condemnation but, of all things, mercy. Without minimizing in the slightest what we have done, he offers us mercy. We can go home now. In fact, he is the home we go to, and he gives us the power to live a vastly different life. Out of this place where we have been loved in our shame, we come to know ourselves as women worthy of love. And this love changes everything.

Knowing yourself as a woman worthy of love is a very different place from which to relate to a man. The secret of most relationships is that others follow our cues. If we have no respect for ourselves, we invite others' disrespect. And if we have been embraced by a love as vast and powerful as the love of Jesus, we will know what to hope for from a man. We will not be willing to take the crumbs from under the table of love.

Betting the Farm

Whatever would mark the dance between men and women is meant to be beautiful. This beauty is built on courage. If there is no real investment in a relationship—no active renunciation of all others, no willingness to sacrifice my interests for yours—the whole affair starts to smell. It quickly wilts and withers. Passion is made of sturdier things, and the foremost among them is courage. Unless we are truly brave hearts, we cannot waltz with a man in a dance worth dancing.

What no one ever actually says out loud is that this delicate, beautiful dance between a man and a woman leads to a cliff. There, dressed in their finest, before an assembled crowd of friends and family, they hold hands and jump together into thin air. *For better or for worse, in sickness and in health, forsaking all others . . . parted only by death.* They promise to love each other in their unlovable moments and to offer respect in times when there is not a heaping lot to admire. They literally bet the farm, and it is right that they do so, because beauty requires this kind of courage. Always.

They literally bet the farm, and it is right that they do so, because beauty requires this kind of courage.

Author Frederick Buechner writes, "They say they will love, comfort, honor each other to the end of their days. They say they will cherish each other and be faithful to each other always. They say they will do these things not just when they feel like it but even . . . when they don't feel like it at all. In other words, the vows they make at a marriage could hardly be more extravagant."[39]

Courage comes in many forms. For many, it takes shape by degrees. I think of a woman, for instance, who felt she needed to make a sharp break in the way she had been relating to men. She felt God was leading her into a place of deeper vulnerability as a woman—the vulnerability of *not* sharing a sexual relationship with the guys she dated. In the past, it had been easier to relate physically to guys—sex kept them happy, and she felt temporarily secure. To check sex at the door and offer a man just "me, myself, and I," required far more guts. Gone was her old sense of feeling in control. Real vulnerability always entails courage.

Moreover, it takes courage to let your sexual life go dormant once it has been up and running. Sex is the convergence of many sensations, an incomparable experience. But when sexual desire is awakened before its time, "desire becomes lust, and lust is restless and shrouded in shame."[40] Eventually the experience itself is spoiled. If you've been "awakened" to sex, then you know that allowing this part of your life to rest, to go dormant, brings questions of real trust and courage: If I let this go, will I experience it again? Will God resurrect the experience of sexual intimacy with the man I marry in a way that will make all I've known seem like a faded postcard from a place I wasn't meant to visit?

And finally, if you have felt burned in your relationships with men, it takes courage to let yourself hope—or hope again—for all the good a man has to give. The makings of romance are hidden in this hunger for the kind of strength and solidity that men bring to your life—something uniquely and wonderfully male that cannot be replicated in friendships with other women. To cup your hands around this flame and protect it from the winds of disappointment until the right man comes along is no small thing; it is an enormous act of courage.

This kind of inner waiting—this willingness to hope—is right at the heart of being a woman who is preparing to enter the dance of her life.

Sexuality and Your Soul

1. When are you struck by the beauty that is possible in a relationship between a man and a woman?

2. How do you sense that sex raises the stakes in a relationship?

3. What would it mean in your life to expect more in your relationships with men?

4. In what ways does forming a sexual relationship before marriage affect a couple's married relationship?

5. Think about the woman who was dragged to Jesus by a mob intent on stoning her for adultery. What stands out in the way Jesus treated her? What in this account draws you to Jesus?

Chapter 6

What Really Happens in Sex

There is no union on earth like the consummation of the love between a man and a woman. No other connection reaches as deeply as this oneness was meant to; no other passion is nearly so intense. People don't jump off bridges because they lost a grandparent. If their friend makes another friend, they don't shoot them both....Troy didn't go down in flames because somebody lost a pet. The passion that spousal love evokes is instinctive, irrational, intense, and dare I say it, immortal.

John Eldredge

The smell of roses gently nudged her out of a deep sleep. Tiny shafts of bright sunlight peered around the curtains beside her bed, and for a minute she struggled to recall where she was. She was slowly being stirred awake. This morning was different from any other she had known, for one noticeable reason. Lying there beside her was a man.

It came back to her in a flood of jumbled images—a wedding and a bad case of nerves, the blur of friends' faces at their small reception, her mother's tears as she left with this man who was now her husband, the flowers in their hotel room. Thinking of the shy awkwardness of their intimacy made her smile. Sex had been nothing spectacular in and of itself. It was a long way from Hollywood to be sure, yet it had been an experience so personal, so deeply altering, it felt like she had woken up on another planet.

She lay her head on her husband's chest, watching the rise and fall, the steady rhythm of his breathing. His arm pulled her closer. She had known him for a couple of years now, yet overnight so much had changed between them. It surprised her how different she felt because of the intimacy she had shared with this man. Something in her had been touched on a level she hardly knew existed. She belonged to someone in a way she never had before. *Maybe this is what it's like to feel married,* she thought.

Waking up the morning after is one of those truly private moments in life when neither your thoughts nor your experience should be up for public display. It belongs to you alone. I write about it, though, as a way of issuing an invitation to explore the mystery of how a man and woman are bonded on a deep level, where trust and naked honesty lay them bare before each other in the experience of sexual intimacy. A bond like no other is begun in this place. If ever there was a human encounter in which more happens than meets the eye, it's sex.

Hearing women talk about their lives has afforded me a kind of window I never thought I'd have into the mystery of sexuality. All the therapy on the planet cannot accomplish what the arms of the man you love can. The insight I've gained comes

If ever there was a human encounter in which more happens than meets the eye, it's sex.

from stories in which, for instance, a woman begins to share how sexual abuse as a child ravaged her sense of self. Or being adopted made her question just how lovable she was. Or perhaps the loss of her father left her grasping for attention and approval. She shares this wound as though it is partially healed, something she has truly begun to move past.

So I ask, of course, how this ache in her has subsided.

"Well, um, I think there's something about the safety, the security, I experience in the physical love of my husband that has really helped me."

She is saying that in the recurrent sexual drama of being held in all her vulnerability in the arms of a man who has pledged himself to her, come what may—something broken, deeper than words can touch, is being healed, piece by tiny piece.

"Oh," I reply, and we both nod our heads, saying nothing more, because words are useless in the presence of mystery.

God is the author of this mystery, so nothing you will ever learn about sex will make much sense without him. The greatest clues to the way God bonds a man and a woman, initially through their sexual relationship, are given in the classic verse used in most weddings, words spoken in Genesis at the dawn of time: "For this reason a man shall leave his father and his mother, and be joined to his wife; and they shall become one flesh."[41] A strong hint to this bonding process is expressed in the word *joined*. The Hebrew for this word means "to adhere." A man and a woman leave their original families and "stick to" each other. The glue, amazingly enough, is sex. Body, spirit, and soul come together in a bond that is meant to grow strong enough to last a lifetime.

Each of us carries an ache inside that seems to be met uniquely through sexual union. "When God created Eve, as you recall, he took her straight from Adam's side. None of us has fully recovered from the surgery. There is an aloneness, an incompleteness that we experience every day of our lives. How often do you feel deeply and truly known?"[42] This deep ache to know and be known is healed at least temporarily through union with another. And from this experience a bond like no other on earth begins to form.

This mysterious glue, this bond, runs far deeper than words, which helps explain why a newly married couple feel they belong to each other in a way they did not the day before their wedding. Or as one young wife in her first few months of marriage told me, "I've noticed that when my husband's neck hurts, it feels like mine does too." The early stages of bonding are just like that— you are becoming so connected to another person that for a while you aren't sure where you stop and he begins. And while bonding exists on many levels, the doorway is primarily the sexual experience. In a cascade of metaphors, Solomon writes about the consummation of his marriage:

> I have come into my garden, my sister, my bride;
> I have gathered my myrrh with my spice.
> I have eaten my honeycomb and my honey;
> I have drunk my wine and my milk.

And God himself responds:

> Eat, O friends, and drink;
> drink your fill, O lovers.[43]

God knew it would take something special between a man and a woman to bear the weight of life together. Bonding means that when you are irritated with your man, when you hate his haircut—even when he does something terribly disappointing—you are still deeply connected. His is the first face you look for in a crowd. My daughter recently asked me a question that gets right at the heart of bonding. "Mom," she said, "do you still think of Dad as a good-looking man?"

Her question caught me totally by surprise. I had to think about that one.

"Well, I know he used to be a good-looking man," I finally replied. "I've always thought of him as a good-looking man."

And I left her question at that. But truthfully I would be no judge of Stacy's looks at all. He could have tractor-trailer tread marks all over his face and I would hardly notice. I have thirty years of bonding—of shared memories, private jokes, and deep connection—with this man.

Even in the physiology of sex, you can see the fingerprints of God and the intentional way he brings a man and woman together. For the first eighteen months of marriage, for example, clinical research shows that couples have elevated hormones coursing through their bodies, providing a kind of "romance cocktail" that makes it very difficult to get to work on time. Sex is the major event, and it happens with stunning frequency. One of those hormones, oxytocin, promotes feelings of closeness and intimacy between two people. And during sex, oxytocin jumps to five times its normal level. Every physical aspect of their being conspires to bring them together and to give them great pleasure in the process. That's how invested God is in bringing a man and a woman together.

> *Even in the physiology of sex, you can see the fingerprints of God and the intentional way he brings a man and woman together.*

A Bond—Whether You Want It or Not

So much more happens during sex than sex. Volumes of meaning are communicated through touch. For many people, sex is the most tangible experience they know of feeling loved and wanted by another person. Sex is a place of grace, not something to be earned like everything else in life. It's a frame that holds a husband and wife together when the days grow dark and no words are strong enough to make everything all right.

I am reminded of the gentle wonder that transpires in sexual intimacy whenever I read a certain rather obscure passage out of the life of Isaac, Abraham's son. Isaac's mother, Sarah, had just died, and the whole community was mourning her death. The book of Genesis gives a touching glimpse of what brought Isaac comfort. "Isaac brought [Rebekah] into the tent of his mother Sarah, and he married Rebekah. So she became his wife, and he loved her; and Isaac was comforted after his mother's death."[44]

Comfort, pleasure, a sense of being deeply known and loved and cared for—who would ever guess that all this is communicated through such a simple physical act. But it is. Can you sense how much God wants to give you in the experience of sexual intimacy? He places such firm boundaries around it because there is so much to be had here. If you can sense the great, good heart of God in this, you will understand immediately one of the strongest, no-nonsense verses in the New Testament: "Marriage should be honored by all, and the marriage bed kept pure, for God will judge the adulterer and all the sexually immoral."[45] God's desire is for you to reserve sexual intimacy as this one place of sanctuary in your life, where nothing defiled, nothing but blessing touches you. And he will not allow anyone to tamper with what he has created without experiencing the consequences.

Sometimes when I read the classic passages of Scripture devoted to sexuality, I find myself a little repelled. Initially they sound so strong, so "in your face." Like the verse just mentioned, sexual sin is often coupled with God's judgment. Those are not the words of a harsh, exacting schoolmaster, however; they are the words of a good Father, better than our wildest imaginings. A good father does not always speak in gentle whisperings and soft nudges. When the issues are big ones, he shouts, "Stop." If a Mack truck is headed this way, he grabs his child by the hand and forcefully pulls him out of the street. Likewise, the Bible uses strong language about sexual sin because sexuality is so much at the core of who we are and who we are meant to become.

I once talked with a woman in her early twenties who had grown up aware that sex was not a recreational pastime, that sex was a sacred encounter. Nevertheless, she was thoroughly convinced she could have sex on her terms. She could walk away with most of the pleasure and little of the pain.

I remember her words as though I had spoken to her yesterday. "I intend to keep sleeping with the guy I'm seeing," she said. "It's that simple. I don't see why sex has to be any big deal. I want what I want."

I said little because the woman's mind was made up. But what ran through my head was, *Honey, you are up against the laws of the universe, and they are bigger than both of us.* And I remembered a few times in my own life when I naively thought I could write the rules.

Whatever noises we may make about God, if we try to write our own script, we will not get far before we hit a wall. God knows we are holding him at arm's length. I love the words of Andy Crouch, the editor of a thinking person's journal that devoted an entire issue to sex. He writes that all of us come to God as "forgiven sinners, still blinking in dazed amazement at grace's invasion of our lives—including our sexual lives."[46] We all wander blindly until the light of God's grace penetrates our own particular darkness. We are "blinking" at this invasion of light that floods every corner, that pierces right to the center of us. And, of course, this light invades our notions of sex and sexuality.

The mystery of bonding in sex is an inviolate one; sex creates a bond whether we want one or not. That's why shame, betrayal, and loss are hard to shake when a woman has slept with a man and the relationship dissolves. Something has happened between them on a level that neither person can "get at." There is, perhaps, no more ironic phrase than the oxymoron *casual sex.*

Women spend a lot of energy trying to convince themselves that sex should not matter so much. They ought to be able to slough it off like so much dandruff on their shoulders. As one woman explained, "I kept watching the way my roommate could just 'do' one man this week and another the next. I tried to become as dispassionate as she was—to treat sex like it was nothing more than frosting on the cake of a great party or a nice dinner out." She was actually relieved to think that maybe she was the normal woman and there was actually something wrong with cutting your heart and soul off from your body.

Women spend a lot of energy trying to convince themselves that sex should not matter so much.

When Mary met Steve, he was leading music in the singles group at her church. Since she was a bit on the shy side, she admired the way he could be at ease in a crowd. Before long they were something of an item. Steve vowed he had never met anyone like Mary.

Neither of them intended for the relationship to get sexual, but it did. Once her affection was sealed, he began to flirt with other women and to be irritated by any show of jealousy or suspicion on her part. It all came to a head when one of Mary's friends confessed that Steve had been calling her, suggesting they go out.

Mary kept trying to work things out, but when she finally realized the relationship was over, she dissolved in a pile of tears and anger. Steve couldn't understand why she felt so disappointed and ashamed. Why couldn't she just go on peaceably? "What's wrong with you?" he asked. "Are you crazy or something?"

The word "crazy" drove Mary's pain underground in a big way. She moved on to other relationships with men, all of which included sex, trying to prove to herself that she was normal— meaning mature and indifferent. But after a while, she started to lose her ability to trust. She felt edgy and insecure with nearly everyone.

I was the first person in Mary's life to say the obvious: "Of course you were crushed. Of course you felt enormous pain." It's totally understandable. You can't share this kind of intimacy with a man and brush it off lightly—not without becoming dead on the inside. The bonding aspect of sex is so real that outside its rightful context it becomes a form of bondage, leaving an imprint on the larger personality that takes time to work through. It affects your ability to trust and your readiness to share your real self with someone in a close relationship.

The same principle holds true in the physical world. If you try to pull apart two objects that have been glued together, parts of one will be stuck to the other. Both will show the scars of being torn apart. The world of relationships is no different. Your heart and soul will follow your body. If a connection to a man is made and broken—made and broken again and again—you may lose your capacity to bond to someone deeply. Like glue that has been squeezed out of a tube, everything inside has been spent and you feel numb.

God, in his mercy, longs to restore our souls. And the truth is that because he authored the mystery of sexuality, only he can restore our souls. Only God can touch the same deep places in you that are awakened in the experience of sex. He made you. The deep places of your soul belong to him first. He gathers up the fragmented pieces of our shattered dreams—of our very selves—and knits them back together, and when he does, it feels like a small miracle.

Being in a Body

Understanding how a man and a woman are bonded in the sexual experience is really built on the significance of the body itself. The mystery hinges on the reality that you and I were given a body, one cell of which is as complex as New York City. We are housed in flesh and blood.

In the educated ignorance of our day, we treat the body as an engine to keep oiled and running. Or as a vehicle that provides us pleasure through eating and sex. Or as a shape we live inside that needs to be sufficiently thin and attractive. And then, when we die, we dissolve into nothingness, or as Beatle George Harrison insisted shortly

> *Understanding how a man and a woman are bonded in the sexual experience is really built on the significance of the body itself.*

before his death, "The universe is a great ocean, and I am a drop of water heading back there."[47]

Christianity is unique in its startling claim that you are far more than a drop of water heading back to the ocean. Your very body is telling you something of the mystery that you belong to a God who made himself known in skin and bones—in Jesus Christ. Think of all the ways God could have chosen to make his glory known. In the Old Testament, he placed his glory in a tabernacle and in a pillar of cloud and fire that led Israel in the desert. When God visited his creation, he could have chosen to dwell in a mountain or a dolphin or a holy book. But God came as a man, in a body. "The incarnation forever hallows the flesh," early twentieth-century British lay theologian Charles Williams once said.[48] The living God revealed himself in a body, and what we do with our bodies matters.

You understand why, for example, when missionaries went to Africa in the 1800s, they built hospitals and not just churches. Bodies were important. And when Christianity took root in Rome, Christians began to bury their dead and not just burn bodies as the Romans had always done. Jesus promised to one day raise our bodies in such a way that we will be able to recognize each other after death.

From this perspective, then, it makes sense that the Bible describes sexual promiscuity as a form of suicide. "Flee from sexual immorality," it says, "All other sins people commit are outside their bodies, but those who sin sexually sin against their own bodies." Promiscuity is like pulling out a gun and shooting off your foot. God lays claim to our bodies as well as our souls. "Do you not know that your bodies are temples of the Holy Spirit . . . ? You are not your own."[49]

So sex is always more than just sex. You and I cannot engage in something with our bodies without our hearts and souls being affected. A man and a woman's passionate longing to be together in a sexual relationship is their greatest clue to how fervently they long for God; the pleasure they bring each other honors him! In most other major world religions, to be more spiritual is to be less sexual, but not so in Christianity.

Our grandparents, who were not nearly as prudish as we think, knew this mystery better than we do. Part of their wedding vows included these amazing words: "With my body I thee worship." Mike Mason wrote these words in his wonderful book about the mystery of marriage:

> Only when we perceive that nakedness is as close as most of us will ever get to seeing God in the flesh, that these poor bodies of ours are the natural (as opposed to supernatural) expression of God's glory, only then can we begin to understand also that sex is the closest thing to touching Him: that is, next to the Eucharist itself.[50]

The Heart of the Mystery

Any mystery worth its salt has a climax that unlocks a secret long sought—one that takes you to the heart of the story and often one that leaves you with just a touch of awe. The mystery of what happens in relationships, specifically in sexual intimacy, is no different. Follow me behind the scenes for a moment so you can see what is rarely recognized but is really happening.

This drama between a man and a woman plays out against a much larger backdrop. God is telling a story here—his story. He wrote this romance in its original form. Ultimately, it is his heart that searches hill and dale for the one he loves. Most of us shy away from the thought, but every page of Scripture says the same thing: *We are the ones he is seeking.* Out of the refuse heap of our lives, he claims us as his own—as his bride. Unbelievably, this is his great joy:

> "The LORD your God is in your midst,
> A victorious warrior.
> He will exult over you with joy
> He will be quiet in His love,
> He will rejoice over you with shouts of joy."[51]

The union of a man and woman is only part of the tale being told. The story behind the story is that this is a picture of the union God desires to have with us. This is the real intimacy we were made for and one day will actually know. Author John Eldredge makes this observation: "God turns the universe on its head when he tells us that this is what *he* is seeking with *us*. In fact, Paul says that this is why God created gender and sexuality and marriage—to serve as a living metaphor."[52] All the imagery of the marriage feast of the Lamb leads here: "'For this reason a man will leave his father and mother and be united to his wife, and the two will become one flesh.' This is a profound mystery—but I am talking about Christ and the church."[53]

Have you thought about sex as a metaphor for something larger—as a clue to the oneness God desires with you? Or do you see some sort of fire wall between sexual intimacy and the worship of God? There are uncanny parallels between the two. Sexuality and spirituality serve as bookends on your life as a woman. They both touch the deepest longings of your heart. One gives profound insight into the other. That's why the Song of Songs, the Bible's unvarnished romance story, is part of the *wisdom* literature of the Old Testament. There are some things about God we will know only through experiencing the love between a man and a woman. And we will never know ourselves or

Sexuality and spirituality serve as bookends on your life as a woman.

know another person deeply without being connected to the God who called us into being. It is all part of the same mystery.

No writer communicated this parallel more clearly than the sixteenth-century poet John Donne. Known in his younger days for vivid love poetry, Donne eventually wrote about God in much the same vein. God, he realized, was the first object of his passion:

> Yet dearly I love you and would be loved fain,
> But I am betrothed unto your enemy:
> Divorce me, untie, or break that knot again,
> Take me to you, imprison me, for I
> Except you enthrall me, never shall be free,
> Nor ever chaste, except you ravish me.[54]

If you did not know this poem was about God, would you not assume at first glance that he was describing love between a man and a woman? But no, Donne is captivated by the larger love story. We are betrothed, lost in an affair with the enemy, he says, hopeless to free ourselves until God enthralls us, until he ravishes our souls with his love.

Reading Donne's sonnet would almost make you blush. For when you stand back and really think about a relationship with a man and a relationship with God, you realize how one mirrors the other. What is worship, for example, without passion and surrender, the laying bare of the soul before God, with whom you have an exclusive relationship? Real intimacy in sex is based on trust and faithfulness. Aren't those the same qualities at the heart of one's relationship with God?

We are never truly free until our hearts are ravished in the love of God. But then, this is what the mystery of sex has been trying to tell us all along.

At the heart of the mystery of sex is a God who pursues you to the end of the earth, not to pin you into submission, but to embrace you at the core of your being with a love beyond that of any man, a love that penetrates your deepest fears and heals your shame, a love that will not let you go. We are never truly free until our hearts are ravished in the love of God.

But then, this is what the mystery of sex has been trying to tell us all along.

Finding the Soul in Sex

For many women who begin to have sex outside marriage, the first clue they have to the soulish nature of it all is pain. You can't explain messy emotions like jealousy and feeling betrayed without there being a real woman in you who longs for more. This awakening is your soul rolling over and crying to be heard.

In their pursuit of a sexually pure lifestyle, most women find that this connection between soul and body is vital. They must move deeper into the mystery to become free of the bondage of immorality. One woman explains how she began to make the connections inside her:

I wish someone had told me there is an incredibly fine line between sensuality and spirituality. That I have this deep, deep place inside of me that desperately longs for God, and that because of this fine line I would often try to touch this spot through sensual means—sometimes through binge eating, hoping that if I cram enough food down, I would hit the spot and feel full and satisfied; or at other times, I'd search for a penis to reach this unreachable void.[55]

At the risk of sounding crude, she explains that facing her sensual desires was crucial, because buried in them was her longing for God. And when she moved in the direction of what she really longed for, sexual purity became a free choice she was making for the first time in her life. Out of a growing intimacy with God, she was making a choice—not against sex— but for the strength and dignity that belonged to her as a woman made in God's image. *That is freedom.*

If there were no larger story, no deep mystery between us and God, there would be no such thing as promiscuity. I could sleep with my husband's best friend and feel no more guilt than when I truly enjoy a slice of banana cream pie. It's just a pleasure to be had.

If there were no larger story, then oral sex would seem no more than exchanging high cards in a good bridge game. But something in us knows that a woman's throat wasn't made to be a receptacle for a man—that it degrades her, that it cheapens the real experience.

If there were no larger story, you and I could stroll down the backstreets of Amsterdam—a culture even more extreme than ours—where women sit in glass storefronts like any other commodity on the open market, half-dressed, waiting to see which men will pay to have sex with them—and we would not be offended. We would not feel nauseous, like we wanted to smash in the glass and take them all home, if there were no larger story.

But there is a larger story. You and I are not generic beings, as though God took a cup of soul and poured it into whatever container he could find. We are women created in his very image—made as women, not men. Something in us will always cry out for this to be honored. We will forever crave the refuge of relaxing in the arms of a man who has committed his heart and his future to us. Something in us knows that the female body we inhabit is truly the work of an Artist, that the same God who created such beauty cares deeply about the beauty of relationship.

If we listen to the true murmurings of our heart, we will be carried at one and the same time to God and to the rightful embrace of our restored sexuality.

Sexuality and Your Soul

1. What part of this chapter has most enlarged your understanding about the role that sexual intimacy is meant to play in a woman's life? How do you feel about what you've read?

2. Where in life do you encounter the reality of the bond that sexual intimacy creates?

3. What would it be like someday to have a sexual relationship with a man that was so free, so absent of

guilt and shame, that you could openly acknowledge God there with you?

4. What impact does it have on you to realize that God pursues you to the end of the earth, not to pin you into submission, but to lavish his love on you?

5. Is the idea that your longing for God is buried in your sensual desires new to you? What are the implications for your life?

Chapter 7

Getting Back Your Heart

I slept with three other men before I was married, but now that I am, I wish that my husband was the only one. Once you find someone you really love—someone you want to spend your life with—the others don't mean a thing. The memories almost make you ill.

Clara, age 27

"But for you who revere my name, the sun of righteousness will rise with healing in its wings. And you will go out and leap like calves released from the stall."

Malachi 4:2

Sexual intimacy could be likened to a treasure chest. Inside is a wealth of desirable things, even beyond the sheer physical pleasure of the experience. There's a sense of refuge and feeling known by someone, moments of oneness that so rival anything on this planet that it's not hard to imagine them as a tiny sample of the union you most desire—union with God himself. Sex is a touch of healing on the very old ache of incompleteness we carry in our broken, solitary selves.

Why, then, all the fuss?

If so much is possible in a love relationship turned sexual, or in a sexual relationship, period, then is God being the ultimate scrooge to place this experience within the bonds of marriage and to prescribe it as a gift for one man and one woman as they move through life together? Isn't this rather like withholding Disneyland from a bunch of orphans who could otherwise go there?

It looks that way at first glance. Certainly a lot of people see sex and all it provides as a natural progression of events, a romantic tryst to which we are entitled as human beings. Everywhere you look there are books and magazines offering tips on how to provide the ultimate sexual experience to make your life complete.

Oh, that they would tell the rest of the story—the morning-after story. The tale of sheepishly walking back to your dorm or apartment, trying to slip in unnoticed. The regret of discovering there is no future with the man, no love to share forever. There is a dark side to the mystery of sexuality, and hundreds of thousands of women could give witness to feelings we never expected to feel.

As much potential as sexual intimacy has in a marriage to bless and bond a couple, it has, outside the union of a husband and a wife, a commensurate ability to create havoc. It brings not life and love but bondage. The phrase often used is "soul tie," meaning that married or not, starry-eyed lovers or casual acquaintances, two individuals are knit together in ways that affect them long after their sexual encounter. Something transpires between them, on a spiritual level at least, that bleeds over into other relationships and other parts of their lives.

When an unhealthy soul tie forms, the relationship breeds not union and fellowship as God intended, but rather control and fear. Those two emotions, control and fear, grow like a virus in the petri dish of immorality. Lisa Bevere points out, "This same principle [of unhealthy soul ties] makes it very difficult for sexually broken or violated women to stand strong in the face of temptation. They have a hard time saying no even when they want to. They are overwhelmed with either lust or guilt, and

Soul ties with men in your past can resurface in totally unexpected ways.

often both. . . . They become victims and a magnet for sexual abuse and promiscuity."[56]

Soul ties with men in your past can resurface in totally unexpected ways. Listen as one woman describes in her journal a period in her late twenties when the sexual connections of her past began to rattle around like ghosts in the cupboard:

> Why on earth am I starting to have these 3-D memories of men I've been with sexually—some of them years ago now? Okay, so I'm lonely these days. I'm stressed. What else is new? But like a recurring viral sore on my lip, these memories take hold of my imagination and I'm gone. Always, it leaves me with a vague feeling of guilt, a hollow dissatisfaction with my life, and a greater sexual hunger. They change my perception of myself toward an inward self-consciousness that slows me down, pulls me away from God and other people—and deeper into myself. I want out. I am plagued with the feeling that I gave away more of myself than I can get back—and in at least a couple of instances, I got more of a guy than I ever really wanted.

This woman is describing a common trinity of emotions that often wash up on the shores of past sexual encounters—feelings of guilt, hollow dissatisfaction that is hard to pin down, and greater sexual hunger, that is, something to fill the void.

Let me offer an example of this kind of bondage from my own life. For years after I married I had the same dream over and over. Always it was my wedding day and I was standing at the end of a long church aisle. Some kind of fog or haze filled the sanctuary. I could not, for the life of me, see the face of the man I was marrying. Who was waiting for me at the front of this church—Stacy or a guy I had dated for four years previous? I stood there helplessly trying to see through the fog. Who was I marrying? The confusion and panic built, and finally I woke up. Always the same sense of relief overwhelmed me as I realized that the man next to me was indeed Stacy. I had married the "right" guy.

I believe that my dream (which has been the only recurrent one of my life) was the result of the soul connection I had forged over four years in a previous relationship. While Stacy and I were both virgins when we married, I knew I had been too sexually involved with this earlier guy. I knew it at the time. The bondage of the guilt I felt—and my inability to break the pattern—were in large part what brought me to Christ. I could not break free on my own.

This is the way a soul tie works in our lives. We think of an old relationship (or relationships) as history. Perhaps we haven't even thought about it in years, but the residue remains. It surfaces in our insecurity, the vigilant bracing of ourselves in fear of being hurt again. It pronounces judgment over our lovableness, as though we don't deserve the affection of a good man. It mutates into a drive to please: "Just tell me what kind of woman you want, and I will become her." Or sometimes, as in my case, it reappears in something as strange as a dream that won't go away. Lingering soul ties from a woman's past have their own ways of becoming visible.

Breaking Free of Bondage

Growing up, Suzanne was known as "the good girl." She was the only first grader who never got "a worm of misbehavior" pinned on her apple, the teenager who drove her friends home safely when they had too much to drink, and the college student who studied way before the test.

When she landed a job in the big city after graduation, her friends warned her: "This is going to be a whole new ball game." She was leaving the warm shelter of a small church college in New Hampshire to join a nationally ranked architectural firm in Chicago. But, hey, she told them, she'd keep her eyes open. This was just too good a career move to pass up.

It truly was an incredible opportunity. With so much business coming through the front door, Suzanne got the chance to learn on the job, with more and more responsibility invested in her. The managing partners called her "the whiz kid." So she did not think twice when one of them invited her to attend a marketing conference with him in New York.

She has replayed the scene in her mind so many times now, always looking for the place where she should have seen what was coming. Maybe it was the second glass of wine at dinner that clouded her judgment. Surely things were getting dicey when he walked her back to her room, but she was totally floored when he suddenly crossed the threshold and then closed and locked the door behind him. What she regrets the most was that she couldn't summon the words "Get out." It just seemed so out of line to say those words to a man you would technically call your boss, and Suzanne had never been one to make a scene.

She couldn't exactly call what happened between them rape. It was a power play to be sure, but one she agreed to as though walking through a dream. She felt as though she had been stung by a stun gun. This man had a wife and three children at home. And here he was, coming on to her.

This was their little secret, he said afterwards. It never happened again, because Suzanne was too smart to let it. She had purchased her education in the fires of regret. The incident was never mentioned between them. They went on from there— boss and employee, seasoned professional and new kid on the block with her eyes wide open. But for Suzanne it was a major turning point. What difference did it make now whom she got involved with? At least that was the way she felt. From then on having a relationship with a man inevitably turned into a relationship that included sex.

One's sexual past can come in many different shapes and flavors. Suzanne's has a flare of the dramatic, a story fit for a novel. Your experience may be a world away from hers. Perhaps you became sexually involved with a guy you really loved and with whom you shared affection and hope for a future together. That is often the case. Somehow things just didn't work out. Or maybe sexual purity was something you came to value only after you lost it—or perhaps after you realized that it was part of having a relationship with God.

When a woman sees a future with a man to whom she longs to be able to give her heart, she may suddenly become aware that her heart is technically no longer hers. It has been scattered in pieces, enjoyed by other men whose faces are preserved only in scrapbooks. As Clara said, once you find someone with whom you want to spend your life, you wish there were no memories of previous men.

So what do you do with your sexual past in order to have a genuine fresh start?

Going Back before You Go On

The concept of what has come to be called *renewed virginity* has attracted great interest.[57] At least in terms of our innermost being, we can recover an innocence of soul, a regathering of our heart, an inner cleansing that brings wholeness. This kind of inner restoration is inherently a spiritual process.

Sometimes when I am talking with a woman who wants a clean start in life, I wish badly that I had a giant eraser in my hand capable of wiping the slate clean in an instant. But the only process that works is really much better than a magic wand or a giant eraser, for it brings women to the only one who can heal and make whole. It isn't complicated, and it doesn't involve any deep probing of your innermost psyche. It is simply a means by which you can come to terms with your sexual history. Almost any sexual act with a man, especially one that involves a degree of nakedness (such as oral sex or heavy sexual intimacy) will feel like a bond that needs to be broken.

It is important to realize that whatever your sexual history is, the power to break free from the past is not in you or even in the process. The power of God is the only force that can set you free. I'm talking about the same quiet-yet-earth-shattering power that raised Jesus from the dead being brought to bear on this one dark corner of your life—a corner God cares deeply about. The apostle Paul had experienced God's power and prayed that believers would know it: "I pray also that the eyes of your heart may be enlightened in order that

> *It is important to realize that whatever your sexual history is, the power to break free from the past is not in you or even in the process.*

you may know the hope to which he has called you, the riches of his glorious inheritance in the saints, *and his incomparably great power for us who believe.*"[58]

In preparation, you may want to spend some time fasting. You will find that fasting is incredibly helpful for focusing the heart on God and breaking spiritual bondages.[59] You may choose to fast from solid food for a day or from a series of meals over a longer period of time—whatever seems appropriate. Through Isaiah the Lord reminded his people of the power of fasting.

> "Is not this the kind of fasting I have chosen:
> to loose the chains of injustice
>   and untie the cords of the yoke,
> to set the oppressed free
>   and break every yoke?"[60]

On the day you choose to deal with your past, set aside at least a couple of hours during which you will not be interrupted. With paper, pen or pencil, and Bible in hand, find a place where you can be alone. When you are finished, you may want to ask a spiritual friend with whom you feel safe to pray with you.

As you begin the healing process, spend some time in praise and worship. Music helps immensely, and reading praise psalms out loud is a classic way to enter God's presence (Psalms 90 to 100 are especially good). Praise and thank God until you can sense that he is right there in the middle of the muck and mire with you. He is, indeed.

Remember that you are not alone in this experience. Jesus is our Advocate before the Father. He is our High Priest "who has been tempted in every way, just as we are—yet was without sin."[61] This means that Jesus, in ways we can't comprehend, knows and understands sexual temptation. He pleads your case before God. He takes the weight of your sin on his own shoulders. He bears the curse of your sin so that you don't have to feel its sting all your days—that you can instead experience the blessing of God.[62]

Your image of God as you enter this time is important. He is not aloof and removed, doling out small pieces of his favor if you say the right words. He too has been waiting for this moment—waiting for you to wait on him, to look for a deliverance that only he can give.

> The LORD longs to be gracious to you;
>> he rises to show you compassion.
> For the LORD is a God of justice.
>> Blessed are all who wait for him![63]

The next part of this process may take a bit of time. The Bible says that the truth will set us free,[64] but sometimes the truth has to be very specific. This is where a pencil and a blank pad of paper come into the picture. The truth you know but don't consciously recognize has a wonderful way of slipping out on paper. As you begin to write, ask God to show you what you experienced and, most importantly, what you came to believe about yourself, about men, and about God in this place where your soul was opened prematurely to another person through a sexual encounter.

Sex is meant to bring about healing in our lives, but expressed in promiscuity, sex (or even pseudo-sex) brings a wounding of some sort—pain that follows on its heels and leaves a hole in our lives. In this wound, a lie inevitably takes up residence. We believe this lie, whether it be about ourselves, about God, or about men. And when this lie sits in our soul and festers, it becomes a lens that alters our perspective. We start to "see" life through the lens of these lies. This is the unholy sequence: *a wound that gives birth* to a lie that turns into a lens through which we see life and relationships in a distorted way.

Write about Each of the Men in your Life

- What drew you into this sexual relationship?

  I think Matt came along at a time in my life when I particularly needed male attention. With my father having left a few years before, it just felt so incredibly good to have a guy single me out. I felt wanted and appreciated for the first time in a long while.

- What was the negative emotional and spiritual impact?

  I tried to go on as though nothing much had happened. But I hated myself for what I'd done with him. I turned kind of hard after Matt, determined that I'd get out before the next man decided to.

  I felt like I was just going through the motions with God—like he was on another planet.

- How did the relationship affect the way you saw yourself and God and other men? (What are the lies you believed?)

  After Matt, I saw myself as a woman who didn't quite have what it took to keep a man interested in her. I was the one left behind, the one who just wanted too much from a guy. I was, supposedly, impossible to please.

*It felt like God wasn't all that interested in
me either! I guess I saw him as not caring
what happened from this point. It was all up
to me to find the love I longed for.*

Some women find they write pages and pages. Others, like
this one, say what they need to say in a few sentences. The part
that surprised this woman was the judgment she passed on herself after she and Matt broke up—she must be a woman who
is impossible to please, who
wants too much from a man.
This is actually the opposite
of the truth. It's the lie she
swallowed in her pain. After
Matt, her real problem was
accepting poor treatment
from guys, taking almost
anything one threw her way.

*This is the unholy sequence:
a wound that gives birth to
a lie that turns into a lens
through which we see life
and relationships in a
distorted way.*

As you can see in what this woman wrote, our pain often
gets projected onto God, as though he caused it or doesn't care.
The worst part of promiscuity is the sense of spiritual and emotional isolation it causes. At the very point where we need the
comfort of a good Father most, we don't feel we can go to him.

Pray about Each of the Men in Your Life

Nothing feels cleaner than a prayer of repentance. Essentially you are laying down the pain, the lies you believed, and
the choice you made to get sexually involved with each man you
have written about. I wish I could convey how much it helps to
pray through what you have written with a friend or a therapist
or a pastor or a spiritual director. Receiving communion is also

an active way of applying the sacrifice of Jesus Christ, his body and blood, to this corner of your life where it is most needed.

Nothing feels cleaner than a prayer of repentance.

What is important is that there is a living, breathing witness to your change of heart, to the breaking of a connection that never should have been. If at all possible, bring someone into the fight with you. The apostle James offers this simple, timeless remedy: "Confess your sins to each other and pray for each other so that you may be healed."[65]

In praying through each of these relationships, you are offering yourself afresh to God so that he can restore the broken places in your soul by his mercy and power. You are asking him on the merits of Jesus Christ to break any remaining ties or bondage in your life from these relationships. You are asking his forgiveness. And because there is nothing more binding to your soul than unforgiveness, you are offering forgiveness to whatever man you may need to forgive.

> *In the name of Jesus and by the power that raised him from the dead, I ask you, Lord, to sever whatever negative spiritual and emotional ties were created in the promiscuity of this relationship.*
>
> *I confess and renounce my sin and the idolatry of preferring any love over yours.*
>
> *I ask you to speak truth to the deepest part of me, and I renounce the lie [name the lie] I believed as a result of this experience. Knowing your willingness to forgive me, I offer this same forgiveness to the man/men with whom I have been involved.*

*I ask your Spirit to cleanse me from every promis-
cuous image, every ungodly thought. Please gather up
every fragment of my soul and make me whole again.
Make me, above all, yours.*

*I praise you for your mercy, and I claim, in Jesus
Christ, the freedom and power to lay hold of my des-
tiny as a daughter of the living God.*

God will lead you as you pray. This is a holy moment in your
life, more significant than you can now imagine. When you have
finished praying about a particular relationship, tear up the
page you have written—or burn it—as a symbolic way of letting
go of the past.

What a woman often finds in this process is that once she
has prayed through the promiscuous aspect of a previous relationship, she is able to retrieve the best parts and take them forward with her. In other words, that Jim made her feel like a
million bucks because he loved her sense of humor, or Dillon
taught her to ski, or Tony opened the world of politics to her—
all these are good gifts she can now keep freely. In a very practical sense, God's heart is always *to redeem*—to reach into the
fire of our own making and by his mercy pull out the good. Only
God can bring blessing where we have sown curse.

When you are finished praying through the relationships
you have written about, you may want to read Psalm 116, a
psalm that amazingly gathers up the pieces of this time. Psalm
116 was obviously written by a kindred spirit; you will recognize his words as the cry of your own heart. Read the psalm
through a couple of times. If you want it to come alive in a special way, try writing it in your own words:

I do love you, Lord, because you hear my prayer.
You turn your ear toward me,
so I will call on you as long as I live.
Death was all around me; my life was a mess.
I had nowhere to turn until I called on you.
You are the one who has saved my life (my paraphrase).

The Door of Hope

Only slowly over time did it dawn on me what the sensuality of my past had cost me. I thought it was something I left behind like a sweater two sizes too small. Years after I married, though, I would have flashes of insight into the awesome overlap between body and soul. I would see this "other altar" I had worshiped at when I was willing to dole out myself in small pieces for the sake of a man's affection. I would see that I had offered my heart to another god.

When you peel back the edges of promiscuity, what stares back at you is the shape of an idol. We are asking a man to serve as a stand-in god who will fill us or rescue us and give our life meaning, if only for a while, through the illusion of love a sexual connection brings. We are preferring another god, in the form of a flesh and blood person, to the intimacy of God. In C. S. Lewis's terms, we are living in a "bent" state. Leaning in toward another, we try very hard to draw our sense of *life* from him.

This is not the way God made us. You and I are created to stand up straight. We are meant to live with our eyes turned toward Jesus to receive all good things from him—even a man. The wonder of the gospel is that it removes the barrier between us and God. He is actually the one who lifts our heads and invites us into life. Two words shed special light on this process of the reclaiming of your heart: *repentance* and *renouncing*.

Repentance means that I agree with God about a particular sin or habit or attitude in my life. I am no longer trying to hide or pretend. I am willing to give my sin over to God rather than repress it and stuff it down inside. Repentance straightens me up. I am *coram deo*, living before the face of God.

Renouncing is an even stronger word and thus is especially freeing. When you pray, "I renounce this habit or attitude or behavior," you are serving notice. It's like saying, "I close the door of my soul to this sin. It is no longer welcome, and whenever it rears its head again, my stated policy is that I will not invite it to have a place in my life."

I used to shy away from such words as "repentance" and "renouncing" until I grasped more of the love and mercy of God in my own life. The crucial thing is being in a place where your face is lifted up again and the shower of God's love is pouring down on your broken soul. His goodness is so lavish, the big questions are, *Am I able to receive from him? Can I allow myself to live in the freedom of knowing myself as a woman accepted and loved by God?* Repentance is meant to open locked gates in our soul.

Our sexual past is not something most of us think of bringing to God in prayer. We hope to keep that sort of thing locked away, especially from God. It doesn't seem that we could survive his gaze on this part of our lives. And this, then, is what makes you feel as though you are in pieces, your sexuality divorced from your spirituality in ways that leave you feeling half alive. Only God's mercy can make you a whole woman again and able to offer your heart to a man you love.

When God's love embraces your shame and regret, it always comes as a surprise. For he meets you, not with the wrath you expect, but with his undeserved kindness. Through the pain you encounter by your own willful choices, he draws you to a place where you can finally—finally—hear his voice. His voice is firm but gentle. He does not point his finger in condemnation. Rather, right in the middle of the mess you have made, he carves a door of hope and pours his very life in and through you. He gives you beauty for the ashes of shame and failure. He makes new.

When God's love embraces your shame and regret, it always comes as a surprise.

From the narrow restraints of our sexual choices, we skip like "calves released from the stall."[66] The whole pasture of our sexuality, as a woman loved by God, is ours again to enjoy and to give.

In a thousand varied ways, Scripture says all this, and never more clearly than the voice of God through the prophet Hosea:

"Therefore I am now going to allure her,
    I will lead her into the desert
    and speak tenderly to her.
There I will give her back her vineyards,
    and will make the Valley of Achor[67] a door of hope.
There she will sing as in the days of her youth,
    as in the day she came up out of Egypt."[68]

Sexuality and Your Soul

1. As you read this chapter, what kind of thoughts and emotions did it evoke in you?

   > fear
   > anger
   > discouragement
   > sorrow
   > regret
   > hope
   > longing

2. How would you describe what a "soul tie," made through some kind of strong emotional or sexual involvement with a man, has felt like in your life?

3. What kind of fallout or residue or effect have you experienced from this soul tie?

4. When do you experience the longing to have a truly fresh start?

5. How would you finish this thought? *When I think about embracing the love of God in this part of my life, I feel _____.*

Chapter 8

Recognizing a Good Man

Victim of love, it's such an easy part
And you know how to play it so well....
You're walking the wire, pain and desire,
Looking for love in between.

From "Victim of Love," the Eagles

As soon as Alexa walked through the door, I knew something big had happened. She looked noticeably different. Her eyes had an unusual intensity to them. She looked as though something wonderful had just happened to her and she was waiting for someone to notice. I looked down for a second and noticed that the cause for the change was evidenced by her ring finger. Alexa had recently become engaged. I hadn't seen Alexa in a year, so I was eager to hear her story.

"Tell me about this guy," I said, congratulating her. "How did this come about?"

The story came tumbling out. Alexa had worked alongside Ben for months in a coffee shop where she worked part time to make extra money. He was between banking jobs. Slowly their friendship had ripened into something more—something she felt she could build a life around.

Then I asked the question that Alexa surely knew I would. Knowing the men in her past and her profound sense of regret and disappointment, what made Ben different? What made her feel that this man was the love of a lifetime?

"Oh—Ben," she said, shaking her head, "You wouldn't believe how well he treats me." Her answer cheered my soul. She began to rattle through a list of descriptors. His strength of character. The spine to stand for his convictions. Loyalty. Compassion. An ability to draw out of her courage she didn't know she had. A hunger for God. Collectively, her descriptors pointed to a guy who was worthy of her respect. She wanted to marry him.

Being free of a physical relationship, she and Ben had gotten to know each other in many other ways, and their relationship had aged slowly over the course of a year like a bottle of fine wine. Alexa's eyes were wide open, and the more she saw of this man, the more she liked what she saw.

Recognizing a Good Man

Alexa's experience is an example of the way promiscuity allows a woman's inner compass to accept the affection of immature men on the sexual prowl, and how this internal set of bearings starts to shift in good ways as her own life changes. It is as though she wakes up and can actually *see* what a particular man is made of. Her sense of "normal" changes. Feeling loved becomes something much more substantial than merely being embraced or desired sexually.

The good work of God in a woman's life resets this inner compass, piece by piece, until her dignity as a woman is restored. No longer is she willing to take the crumbs, to scrape the bottom of the love barrel. The bar rises on her expectations for a man. Hope works its magic—it helps her discard the mediocre because she senses that God has something better for her. Like a magnet, "good" men are drawn to her positive expectation and lesser men go where they can get what they want quicker, with less required of them.

My point is that we each carry around a compass that points us, as women, in the direction of certain kinds of men. Having this compass set in the right direction determines the men we are drawn to—and the men we attract. Many factors come into play in the setting of this compass—our history with the first man in our life (our father), our first experiences with guys, the places in relationships where we have felt hurt. Our inner compass substantially affects our perspective on men.

Visit with me for a moment some of the memories and images that may affect the way you see men. For instance, can you remember sitting on your father's lap? Did you, like so many girls, get your dad to teach you how to shoot a hoop or throw a baseball? Who was the first boyfriend who brought you flowers? Was there ever a man you loved who held you when you cried—and just holding you was purely enough?

In very good ways, those kinds of memories shape an expectation inside you that serves like a compass to keep you pointed in the direction of men you can trust—men who will offer their strength to shelter you and to do you good. "True north" in the world of relationships is always about the best God has put in a man brought together with the best God has put in you—for a purpose larger than you both.

> *"True north" in the world of relationships is always about the best God has put in a man brought together with the best God has put in you—for a purpose larger than you both.*

As God restores the integrity of your heart, you will find that your orientation to men changes in significant ways. God teaches you what to look for in a man. Isaiah wrote about the way God personally leads his children:

"I am the LORD your God,
   who teaches you what is best for you,
   who directs you in the way you should go."[69]

In other words, God retrains our thinking about what is truly valuable in a relationship and promises to lead us in the way we need to go.

How the Compass Is Set

When you think about what you have come to anticipate in men, there is no more important man in the picture than your father. Even if you never knew him, or if he left your life through death or desertion, your father is the first man in your life.

We look into our father's eyes as a mirror that tells us we are lovely and valuable as a daughter and as an emerging woman. This begins very early. I remember, for instance, noticing when our daughter turned three how differently she related to Stacy—the innocent thrill of being Daddy's girl, her squeals of delight as she was hoisted above the world on his shoulders.

For most of us, our father is the man we first get to "try out" our femininity on.

For most of us, our father is the man we first get to "try out" our femininity on.

What you did or did not experience with your father shaped your hope for what you could expect to experience with any man thereafter. He laid down the grid you carried out into the larger world.

There are many women these days who by the age of thirteen lost their fathers through death or divorce and now realize how that loss propelled them into the arms of whatever guys crossed their paths. Indeed, the tender years of turning from a girl into a young woman are a deeply formative time for the protection and valuing of our sexuality. Many of us later see that accepting the sexual advances of a boyfriend was a poor substitute for wanting a really good talk with Dad.

I don't mean to imply that we can pass off responsibility to our fathers for the poor choices we have made regarding men. We have to own the choices we have made in order to make new ones (for example, "I'm the one who decided to spend the night at John's apartment when I was eighteen"). While a father's absence may shape the hole in our soul, we choose how we will fill it.

Every father, no matter how good or how poor, falls short in some way. Some fail dramatically. We have places of aching need in our soul that even the best father cannot humanly touch. The question that shapes our lives is *where* we take this need. Many of us envision redemption in the shape of a man— a living, breathing person very different from ourselves who seems destined to fill the void.

When I was in my early twenties, I came upon a startling promise in this regard in the book of Psalms: "My father and my mother have forsaken me, but the LORD will take me up."[70] In other words, if my parents abandon me literally, or if they simply fail me as human beings, God promises to "take me up" in my orphaned state. He will become both father and mother, in the deepest sense of the word. He will do what no man in my life can do.

Growing up, then, whether you are twenty or fifty, is mostly about switching fathers. Your real Father spoke the world into being, yet he also has your name engraved on the palm of his hand. He knows when you lie down and when you arise. He records your tears in his book. Like the best of all possible fathers, he pours the healing oil of his love, if you let him, into the hole in your soul.

How Do You See Men?

We have seen that each of us carries an internal compass that governs the kind of men we attach to, what we are conditioned to expect, and how we interpret feeling loved. Loving a man sexually and then leaving him or being left by him has a profound effect on our psyche. The repeated making and breaking of sexual bonds tilts our inner compass noticeably off the mark. Let's explore three common distortions that are birthed in relational pain.

> *Each of us carries an internal compass that governs the kind of men we attach to, what we are conditioned to expect, and how we interpret feeling loved.*

An Impossible Dream

Sometimes when a woman's past is littered with broken relationships, she becomes drawn like a magnet to "the impossible man"—the guy who's really not capable of offering anyone much of a relationship. One good conversation, maybe two, and a woman's most appropriate response would be, "Next?" It's time to move on.

Sometimes a woman's past predisposes her toward men who are fundamentally inaccessible. Sarah grew up with a father she greatly admired but who was always emotionally out of reach. She could never just sit and carry on a conversation with him. The men Sarah became attracted to were charming and flirtatious; for a while, being with them made Sarah feel like the belle of the ball. But when you scraped off the veneer, the man himself was utterly self-absorbed. He was on again, off again—there only when he felt like it. Sarah, however, was so busy doing his part and hers, convinced that her love could heal him, that she barely noticed his poor behavior until she was way into the relationship.

As Sarah began to recover her own soul—as God set things right on the inside of her—she began to explore the nature of *friendship*. What did a give-and-take reciprocity look like in any relationship? What did it mean to stand back and watch a man until she could see his heart and he had time to prove his worth or lack thereof? Finding true north, for Sarah, involved exploring these questions.

The other thing that radically changed for Sarah was her definition of "exciting." What she previously called exciting was the breathless way she felt when she had been jerked around. A quote from Robin Norwood's vintage *Women Who Love Too Much* explains this transition best:

> She had to learn to simply be in the company of men whose company she considered nice, even if she also found them a little boring . . . no bells peal, no rockets explode, no stars fall from heaven. . . . Because she was used to excitement and pain, struggle and victory or defeat, an interchange that lacked these powerful components felt too tame to be important and unsettling as well.[71]

A Source of Life
The ending of a relationship (even if you are the one who let go) can make the object lost compulsively desirable. Many

women go from one man to the next out of a terrific fear of being alone. Alone is just not doable. It means that you are unwanted, unloved—you are standing out in the cold with your nose pressed up against the warm pane of unattainable intimacy. Only a man can make the solitariness go away.

Seeing the other gender as the source of life is a temptation that goes all the way back to the Garden of Eden. You can sense it in the bony, blaming fingers that Adam and Eve pointed at each other. The thinking is, *Somehow, if a man [or a woman] were just here for me in the way I need, my life would be okay.* All the while, someone is present who knows and understands our solitariness so well that his most common response is, "Do not fear, for I am with you." God has promised to take the toxic awfulness, the shame, out of being "alone."

Suppose the frame around being without a relationship was different. Suppose this was a providential season to get your own stuff together and to discover life—to enjoy the people around you, to get to know God better. Aloneness can be nontoxic, open space in your life filled with a world of possibility. So many women say after they wrestle their fear of aloneness to the floor, that a string of months—or a couple of years—with no man in their life was the best thing that ever happened to them. It gave them "just me" time for their own personal growth.

Coming into a relationship with a man from the emotional vantage point of knowing deep in your soul that you are already loved is liberating. Before any man appeared in your life, you were loved by God. You were given worth and honor by the only one truly worthy of such. To embrace this is to be set free. When you can look at a man and know that he can't give you what you most long for—worth and love and a sense of identity—then you are free to be loved by him. The most he can ever do (which, in itself, is no small thing) is to give witness to the worth God already invests in you. But you must claim it first for yourself.

I am often drawn to the words of a man who spent his life as a single man—the apostle John. In the simplest of phrases, he described himself as "the disciple whom Jesus loved."[72] The love of Jesus was that real to him. Can you imagine being able to describe yourself simply as a woman whom Jesus loves? It is his love that makes the situation of being alone, without a relationship, one that holds its own share of possibilities and life.

Merely a Useful Appendage

The other common distortion is almost the opposite of feeling that life doesn't begin until there is a man in one's life. It is the mentality that men are expendable and we are above needing one for any reason.

Women have worked hard not to need men in some of the obvious ways they used to need them. More and more, they have their own paychecks. They own homes, fix the plumbing, mow the grass, and maintain their own cars. They get used to playing hardball with the guys every day in a work setting. It's great to be able to do the things men do well—unless it starts to seem as though your world is stuck there and your softer, more vulnerable side gets lost.

If you add a broken heart into this mix, you can end up perilously close to seeing men as merely a useful appendage. Some women may say, "Men. Who needs them? They are just one of life's add-ons—useful, especially, if you want children down the road. But I'll just concentrate on succeeding in my career and cultivating my own version of the ya-ya sisterhood." The strong, independent single woman has become a cultural icon.

Oddly enough, in Christian circles, "not needing anyone" is sometimes mistaken for a virtue, as though godliness were about looking to God alone, without any real human touch. But this defies God's plan for you as a woman created for connectedness, with a heart full of longing. It blinds you to the special symmetry that is possible in the presence of a man—no matter what the setting. What he brings to the table and what you bring to the table is, indeed, a sum greater than either part.

Seeing men as something you can do without is usually a response to pain of some sort. Your heart got shut down somewhere along the way. Opening yourself to wanting a man's touch on your life again can feel a bit scary, because doing so carries the possibility of being hurt. Somehow, though, the restorative work of God in a woman's life inevitably leads to this vulnerability that is a part of experiencing real love.

Enjoying the Presence of a Real Man

Jasmine met the guy she first slept with in a church youth group in high school. They had not meant to have sex, but once done, there seemed to be no way back. Besides, they both thought they might eventually want to marry.

What ensued was three years of on-again, off-again attachment during which neither could go forward toward marriage— or backward toward friends. Jasmine grew more and more convinced that she wanted to move on, but something about the physical connection kept her in a place of emotional dependency she found hard to break. Normally a strong person, she got so she could not picture herself alone without this particular guy.

Jasmine says that when she finally broke off this relationship ("Please don't call me anymore"), she entered a period she could only call grieving, similar to what one feels when they lose a spouse to death or divorce. She sought refuge in every other friendship she still had, and she gave herself to growing spiritually. Still it took time to heal.

I have heard innumerable stories like Jasmine's. And it does make sense that a deep connection with a man, one that has been formed sexually, will take time to get past. It's like putting your heart in the hospital and giving God the time required to mend it.

If you find that you need time to heal from a relationship, or if you realize that your choice in men comes more out of desperation and pain than it does wisdom, try spending a season of time with no man in your life. Immerse yourself in a relationship with a very different man, one who will never let you down—the Son of Man, Jesus. He is more real than anyone you or I will ever share a meal or a bed with.

I can promise that you will be safe in his company as have women throughout the ages. You will be valued, protected, and enjoyed. During his years on earth, the women who followed him were a potpourri of everything imaginable. One of his favorites, the first woman to witness his resurrection, had been plagued by demons before she knew his healing touch. Another was the talk of the town, and for good reason. She had known, in the biblical sense, at least six men in her life. Jesus gave her what no man could—a new start and a new identity. Even women like Joanna, whose husband managed the king's business affairs, left her important social life behind so she could follow Jesus from place to place, contributing to his support.

The best explanation for the devotion of these women is that no one ever loved them like he did. Innumerable women would echo just that: "No one ever loved me like Jesus."

There is something incredibly attractive about Jesus as a man. There has to be, because throughout the ages women who feel like cast-off rejects, who fear they've screwed up their lives beyond recognition, have found the shelter of a huge rock in Jesus Christ. They can finally come home.

> *There is something incredibly attractive about Jesus as a man.*

This is the time in your life to let yourself get to know him. He can be found primarily in prayer and in the books of Matthew, Mark, Luke, and John in your Bible. There he walks the pages as God who came to earth as a man. Getting to know him is mostly about letting him in—letting ourselves be loved by him and giving over to him the things that fascinated us while they stole our very life, offering us no true sweetness and no real joy.

It is in simply *being* with him that we are restored and made whole again. He is jealous for your love. His purifying gaze will heal even as it penetrates your soul. He is True North, the one who resets your inner compass such that when a man comes along who even remotely resembles him, you will know.

1. How would you describe the men to whom you have been attracted? What is good about it, and what differences would you like to see in terms of where your "compass" has been set?

2. How has your experience with the first man in your life—your father—affected your expectations of men or the way you relate to men?

3. What do you value and appreciate in a friendship with a man?

4. How would your relationship with a man be different if the experience of being loved by God was more real to you?

5. What tempts you most to develop an attitude of viewing men as expendable?

6. Suppose you took a break from relationships with men and devoted the time to your relationship with God. What would you most want to ask God for during this season? What would you long to experience with him?

Chapter 9

Giving Yourself Away

Sexuality is not simply about finding a lover or even finding a friend. It is about overcoming separateness by giving life and blessing it.

Ronald Rolheiser

$\mathcal{T}$he movie *Antwone Fisher*, which told of an enlisted sea-man's search for his real family, caught the public eye soon after its release. Antwone's tragic flaw is a boatload of anger that stems from an abusive childhood and causes him to use his fists to speak his mind. The movie also storyboards the double mes-sage our culture sends regarding sex, for the brawl that finally lands Antwone in jail is sparked by an insult one of his ship-mates hurls his way in a bar during shore leave. He dares to call Antwone a *virgin*. His dark secret is exposed, and he is humil-iated. Now everyone knows—Antwone is twenty-five years old and has never been with a woman.

Antwone's psychiatrist (played by Denzel Washington) treats Antwone's virginity as evidence of his lack of mental health, a condition in need of curing. When Antwone finally sleeps with his girlfriend, Denzel congratulates him as though he has just graduated from college.

What a turn of events that something as valuable as virgin-ity could take on the aura of a taboo. The strange twist in a sex-ualized culture like ours is that those who exercise restraint feel like the deviant ones, the odd ducks. Yet this is where we are. What does it mean when you choose sexual freedom in the form of boundaries that leave the richest physical experience between a man and a woman to marriage? Moreover, how do you shut the door on sex without shutting down as a woman?

These are the questions that women who remain single for a number of years grapple with—and I confess that I listen with more than a little humility when they talk. I recognize that I have not slept alone in quite some time. And I would be the first to agree that sex itself is pretty good stuff. A woman's choice to forgo an active sexual life and to live in celibacy for the sake of her own freedom and sanity is no small thing.

I am grateful, though, for the earlier experience of pulling back from the edge sexually myself. I know what it is to feel alone and okay walking out into the world, unattached to any man. It is so different to experience a relationship, then, that grows out of friendship and respect that has not been cata- pulted forward via the sexual. It places the decision to marry on much firmer footing. You know this man in so many varied ways that knowing him sexually is just one more piece—albeit a very good one. I count it as one of the great undeserved graces of my life to have a sexual bond with my husband rooted so deeply in trust.

Having said this, though, let me share some thoughts and insights that have come from helping single women navigate relationships once a sexually pure lifestyle becomes their intent.

Courage is required. Sex is much like any other physical appetite in life. Once you have tasted chocolate, you tend to want more. If you have grown accustomed to running a couple of miles a day, your body feels like it is missing something if you aren't pounding the pavement. And if sex has been an ongoing part of your life and a pleasurable one, it takes real courage to let go of this experience of intimacy, for the time being, until God returns it to you in its rightful form. That's why Solomon, in the one book of the Bible devoted to romance and sex, repeats this wise caution three times, "Daughters of Jerusalem, I charge you . . .: Do not arouse or awaken love until it so desires."[73]

There is a time to awaken love, God says. And conversely, awakening love in the wrong context means that appetite has to be lulled back to sleep.

Some feel that one reason God has enabled such a richness in praise and worship music in our day is to provide a vehicle that can carry us into his presence where a greater love envelops us.[74] God knew we would need a way to come to him by which lesser passions could be swallowed up by a greater passion. In letting go of physical intimacy, we are deepening our intimacy with him and trusting his heart to restore our hope for a future better than we could create by our own devices. As author Lisa Bevere writes, "Holiness is not God asking us to be 'good'; it is an invitation to be 'His.'"[75] We belong to him. The best synonym for holiness is the word "freedom."[76]

> *Awakening love in the wrong context means that appetite has to be lulled back to sleep.*

For anyone, it takes time and commitment for sexual appetite to calm down. Thankfully, it won't leave in any permanent way. Sexual pleasure will be there waiting—waiting to be reawakened, hopefully, in a whole new context with a man and a future shared together. But the pull of the flesh is strong. That's why the biblical admonition is a simple one: Flee.[77] Run in another direction. Give yourself to the company of those who are actively pursuing God. This is the very opposite of the "going on a diet" mentality some associate with abstinence. Rather, the energy that would have been siphoned off in sex gets invested in other ways. Life opens up to you in different ways, like a smorgasbord of opportunities that leads to growth.

A change in motivation is necessary. When a woman's orientation to relationships starts to change and connection to a man is about everything except exchanging sexual favors, new questions emerge for her. Her sensitivities are awakened in other areas. She starts to see her own motivations more clearly.

A veterinarian in her late twenties helped me follow the way a woman's motivation in relationships can radically change once sexual games aren't the focus of attention. Cynthia claims that she never really saw how she used sex as a way to guarantee relationship—until sex wasn't in the picture. At first she felt insecure around a man. Being sexually intimate had been a way to feel in control. Her needs for closeness and male affirmation had been met in sexual ways, and her ego received a consistent stroke—even though she hated the way things fell apart later.

Forgoing a sexual relationship opened her eyes to the sheer selfishness governing her life with men. She had lived in relationships like any good consumer, asking herself, "What am I getting? What's in this for me? How can I get this guy to give me what I need?" Cynthia feels that celibacy is what led her to her first taste of real freedom with men. "I discovered the pleasure of being with a guy without trying to manipulate his affection," she explains. "I have learned, as a woman, how to enjoy a man without trying to hook him."

God has given women enormous power in their sexuality. Used in a selfish context, this power mutates into the form of a seductress. The book of Proverbs warns men repeatedly of falling under the spell of the woman who uses her beauty to lure him into an illicit relationship.[78] As destructive as this is for a man, it steals everything good for a woman as well. Where there is no real freedom, there can be no true choice for love either. And love is what we all long for.

Shutting the Door without Shutting Down

Those of us who advocate the fullest of sexual expression within the narrowest of constraints, the marriage relationship, know that we are walking a fine line. Messages of "Just say no" to sex are sometimes said or heard with such negativity that sexuality itself gets covered in shame. All that is feminine and beautiful and attractive gets locked down tight, stuffed in a back closet somewhere, and labeled "bad." When this happens in a woman's life, God's heart is grieved, for nothing on the planet is more essentially our birthright than our sexuality—the pleasure and beauty of being female.

Living as a woman with a sexually pure lifestyle, without unsexing yourself, backs quickly into the larger canvas of what it means to be sexual—and what it means to be female. The issue is deeper than having sex or not having sex. The real questions are ones most of us face at one time or another. What do we do with unmet desire? How is the expression of myself as a woman experienced in a larger sense than sex itself?

Friends who are single and who have wrestled with these questions well and deeply have provided real insight into both. They refuse to let our culture reduce their femaleness to what they provide sexually, as though to rob them of a package far more multifaceted than the delivery of sex. One friend, in particular, tells a funny, sad story to which many women relate:

*Was that my problem—
I just wasn't gettin' any?*

One day when I was teaching high school English (fifth period—I shall never forget this class), I was in a particularly foul mood. Truly, that class could have put a veteran master teacher in a foul mood, but it was particularly tortuous for me, a twenty-five-year-old brand-new teacher. I do not remember the exact sequence of events, but I know it culminated with a kid I'll call Jimmy (greasy, long hair, repeating tenth grade, wearing tight, skinny jeans) who stood up and yelled, "I know what Miss Gillam's problem is: She ain't gettin' any!"

Amazingly, the class went absolutely silent—something they never did. His words shocked even them. Finally, Misty, a tough cookie in her own right, but one who'd come over to my side, said, "Shut up, Jimmy. Sit down."

I took one moment to assess the situation, decided Misty's words, still echoing, were enough, and moved forward as if nothing had happened. But it took a whole lot longer to shake it off inside.

Was that my problem—I just wasn't gettin' any?[79]

What a haunting question. My friend admits there are moments when, like anyone, she longs for "warm flesh against warm flesh," the simple human comfort of physical touch. Though she is far too alive as a woman for this fear to be rational, she confesses a recurring nightmare of waking up one day shriveled, living with a bunch of cats and wearing a beige cardigan as she rocks in her favorite chair. This question of gettin' some or not gettin' some is a live issue to her. It has driven her past the question of sex into the real nature of sexuality itself.

Amazingly enough, excellent insight into the larger question of sexuality comes through the writings of a Catholic priest by the name of Ronald Rolheiser. What he writes about sexuality *in the absence of a sexual relationship* far outweighs the wisdom of those who do not sleep alone. Rolheiser explains that the word "sex" has a Latin root, the verb *secare*, which literally means "to cut off" or "to sever." It speaks to our awareness from birth of being disconnected from the whole—lonely, cut off, severed from others.[80] Thus, in both the sexual act and in our sexuality, our desire is to reconnect—to overcome our incompleteness.

Our culture is fixated on the act of sex, and as a result, we miss the larger picture of sexuality. As great as sex itself is, sexuality is something more. It is this all-encompassing energy inside us that drives us out into the world in a creative, life-giving way. It moves us toward unity and consummation with that which is beyond us.

The accusation that my friend's irritability was the result of "not getting any" led her into a deeper search as to what her sexuality was about. She concluded, paradoxically, that what keeps men and women alive as sexual beings grows out of what they are giving of themselves. It's not what a person is getting or not getting that matters—it's what he or she is *giving*. By this truer standard, for example, even Mother Teresa could be called an erotic woman. She grew wrinkled and old, to be sure—but she did not dry up. In the giving of herself, she was one of the most alive women of her time. As Rolheiser explains, "A mature sexuality is when a person looks at what he or she has helped create, swells in a delight that breaks the prison of his or her selfishness, and feels as God feels when God looks at creation."[81]

The path through the forest, as my friend has found, comes out of the paradox of owning her desire—without narrowing the expression of her femaleness to sex. She has learned to let herself enjoy the fact that men find her attractive—without having to go *there*. She is not running in place, keeping life on hold until she is married. She has found that it is useless to try to fulfill sexual hunger in illicit ways. They do not satisfy. The hole in her soul only gets larger. Even though she has some genuine unmet needs, she feels that wrestling with the crucible of sexuality has not undone her as a woman—rather, it has made her.

Coming Alive

We live in a chaotic time in which the old road maps to being a man or a woman don't seem to work. The important cues are still there, hidden in our members, but it takes longer and we work harder to find the way. Men and women no longer marry upon college graduation, like clocks programmed to strike twelve at the same time. Many more of us are single— some by choice, many unintentionally. The right man just has not come along yet.

In the wake of unmet desire, the woman who "plays by the rules" sexually and yet remains single can sometimes feel resentful, as though she has not seen the payoff. Even worse is the woman who interprets her singleness as punishment for some era of promiscuity in her past. Both of these responses miss painfully the larger cultural picture of what is happening in our day. Neither fits the truth of the matter. Finding a man is not a reward that comes to virtuous women necessarily—or to women who have resolved all their personal issues. If that were the case, none of us would be married.

I talked with a woman recently who married at thirty-eight and had her first child at forty. She had wanted to be married much sooner. "Now I look back," she says, "on the rich experiences I had when I was single—the travel and friends, the hobbies I pursued, the luxury of uninterrupted time with God—and I am so grateful for those years that I kept praying to get past. I wouldn't want anything different."

The truth is that every woman I know, myself included, lives with some very real unmet needs in her life—ones that tug at her heart daily. It may be childlessness, a dead-end career, a difficult marriage, or a host of other open wounds—but trust me, it's there. No one comes through this life unscathed.

Every woman I know lives with some very real unmet needs in her life—ones that tug at her heart daily.

All of us face the same essential choice in life. We can shut down inside, clamp off the pain of unmet desire, and live in a small place where we feel almost nothing. Plenty of women make this choice, often unconsciously. It feels safer than taking the risks that "having a life" entails, but it is really a form of dying on the vine.

To move more courageously, you have to hold on to hope, knowing there are no guarantees how your life story will read. You hold on to hope, and you *trust* that God has a better script for your life than you could write on your own. Married or not, childless or with a house full of little feet, at the top of your field or amazingly average—God's blessing is on your life because the gospel of Jesus is real and true. And if it is true indeed, then you refuse to dull your heart, because being half alive is not what you were made for. You choose to live from the inside out, offering yourself in a hundred good ways to the people God brings your way.

The second path is harder. Anyone will tell you this in a heartbeat. But it leads somewhere worth going, and this makes all the difference. To live in the rarer air of the in-between— neither shutting down desire nor demanding it be fulfilled in a particular way—is your own heart's journey in what it means to trust God with your life. The disease to be feared is not, as our culture claims, that somehow we won't "get any." The real fear is that you and I will go through life holding back the life God has put in us, playing it safe. We'll miss "giving it."

The pain of unmet desire can actually enlarge our hearts. The more we let ourselves long for life though it brings the ache of incompleteness, the more we are actually able to savor the joy that comes our way. This paradox surprises me on a daily basis. More and more, I recognize this kind of pain for what it is—a ticket to becoming a woman so thoroughly alive that she is afraid of almost nothing.

—— *Sexuality and Your Soul* ——

1. What, to you, is the challenge of walking out into the world alone and unattached to a man?

2. How do you respond to the thought that your sexuality is the energy that drives you out into the world in a creative, life-giving way?

3. In what way does sexuality "break us out of the prison of our selfishness"?

4. In what ways have you come to see living with a desire that remains yet to be fulfilled as something that embodies hope, not just disappointment?

5. How would leaning in the direction of hope affect your life?

Chapter 10

The Good Relationship

Human beings always cast ahead of themselves into the morrow, and they bring along with themselves their yesterdays. The self does not fully give itself—however fervent the act—if it withholds the future.

William F. May

When Lynn's friend wanted to set her up with a guy named Jeff Mason, Lynn just rolled her eyes. She knew Jeff from a distance, and he wasn't her type, plain and simple. So Lynn played it safe—she agreed to meet Jeff for a cup of coffee.

The problem was that she had a much better time with Jeff than she expected.

They talked like old friends. She had more fun, just plain fun, than she'd had with any guy she could remember. That was the other part of the problem—there had been a good many guys before Jeff.

Lynn had grown up as the "responsible child" in a family with six children and a mom who worked two jobs trying to make ends meet. The first guy she slept with was a man she met in a bar the summer she turned nineteen. The attention he showed her was like candy to a starving kid. Six months later she felt stung as she watched him do the same number on another girl—at the same bar no less. Soon after, she moved out of state, and in her newfound independence, she had a number of one-night stands that pain her to recall. Her career took off, and by age twenty-six, she met a man she thought she could build a life with. Two years into their marriage, he cheated on her.

All this time, Lynn was vaguely aware of God as though he were a rather imposing figure standing mute on the edge of her consciousness. But there was nothing that could be called a relationship. "Don't count on anyone but yourself" was the creed her mother had taught her. Lynn didn't need anyone. She most surely didn't need God.

After Lynn's divorce, she started dating a man who seemed more promising. While they lived together, he took her to church. Within a few months, Lynn gave her life to Christ, though she admits that she went home and cried for three days, suddenly awake to the scary realization that fundamentally she was divorced and alone and living with a man—the future did not look good. She only knew one way to do life—her way—and she knew only one way to relate to a man. None of it had made her happy, but she had no idea how to do things differently.

Slowly, Lynn began to grow spiritually, drawn by the love of Christ. God put his finger on areas of her past she needed to let go of, one by one—and promiscuity with a man was the last major one Lynn relinquished. When yet another man cheated on her, Lynn realized she needed a sabbatical from relationships. By now she was thirty-five years old. "For six months God and I dated exclusively," Lynn explains. "For the first time in my life I was content and happy with myself. It was amazing."

Then she had coffee with Jeff. And then, as these things go, she had another cup. And another. Lynn admits that for a while she didn't know what to do with a man who treated her so well. It was a brand-new sensation to feel respected—like this guy was genuinely interested in *her*—with no angles. Jeff could see beyond the mess she had made; he brought out the best in her. The analogy Lynn uses is that, before Jeff, she had a "love box" filled with all the false ways she had learned to feel loved by a man. Jeff dumped out the box and began to fill it with something much purer—something a lot more like the love of God.

Lynn and Jeff began to see each other regularly, but they credit a friend with moving their relationship to a new level. "So," the friend asked Jeff, "are you just dating or are you actually courting Lynn?"

"What's 'courting'?" Jeff asked in all innocence. Being Australian by birth, Jeff thought this might be another American invention.

"Oh, you know," the friend replied. Then she offered a very unconventional means of romantic involvement. "Courting is when you give a woman a quarter each time you see her, and the great fun is to see where she finds it. You *court her* with *quarters.*"

Thus began a romantic surprise that came hidden in nearly every date. Lynn might find a quarter in her shoe, or under her dinner plate, or waiting for her on a chair. She never knew. What she did know was that every time she found a quarter, Jeff had thought about her. Something wonderful was starting to happen between them. On the evening Jeff asked Lynn to marry him, he began by giving her a quarter he had framed. The inscription read, "This is the last quarter I hope to give you." They married six months later.

Lynn and Jeff are quick to say that deciding to save physical intimacy until they were married was particularly hard because "they'd been there" before with others. For Lynn especially, sex meant the deep reassurance that she was loved. She remembers praying one morning early in their "courting" and words forming in her brain as clear as though she had heard them out loud: *Do . . . not . . . sleep . . . with . . . this . . . man.* God could not have made it clearer to her that *this* relationship was to be different from all the others. She and Jeff made a vow together to wait until they were married—a pledge that sent Jeff running out the door on occasion. But this same vow also led to a very sweet season of romance and playfulness. "It was a whole new kind of freedom," Lynn says. "I felt loved and respected and honored in the purest sense."

Allowing physical intimacy to follow marriage rather than precede it feels like an investment that Lynn and Jeff are still cashing in on. "To be sure, I wish Jeff had been the only man I'd been with," Lynn says. "But the struggle and commitment to wait have built a real solidity in our relationship." She notes that when they argue and the air gets tense, it never crosses her mind that Jeff will leave. Something very strong has been forged between them.

Lynn and Jeff have been married four years now. They are parents of a daughter almost two years old. "Sometimes when I look in my daughter's eyes," Lynn explains, "I am bowled over by the mercy of God."

Building a Relationship on Trust

In a day when the signals between men and women are not so clear, it is hard to tell when you have come upon a special connection with a man—or as they say, when the man himself is a "keeper." As Lynn's story suggests, sometimes a man you might never expect can turn out to be the love of your life.

Sometimes a man you might never expect can turn out to be the love of your life.

But how would you know? A man does not come with a tag that says, "Trust me. I won't let you down." There is no machine that takes an X-ray of the heart. Oh, people will tell you that a good relationship means that two people have common interests and similar values. They will ask you if, indeed, you are physically attracted to this guy (in other words, he does not *just* seem like a good brother). A paycheck is always nice. The hope of future paychecks is especially nice. He may have the blue eyes you always dreamed of and the manners your mother thinks are indispensable in a man. You may feel like the luckiest woman alive when you're with him. But none of these things are enough. And all of it put together does not get at the elusive quality that all good relationships have in common.

In other words, you can't build anything with a man for the long haul that is not infused, through and through, with *trust*. Trust is the root from which love flowers and continues to bloom. How you answer the question "Can I trust this man?" will determine whether you feel you can give your heart in any significant way.

But trust is hard to explain. It's almost something you come to sense in your gut. For some time now, I have taken it upon myself to interview women on the question of how, exactly, they came to know they could trust the man they married. Or in the case of one single woman, I asked her how she separated the men she could take home to her father from the fish she threw back in the pond. The responses I received are worth a small book itself.

Does He Mean What He Says?
As simple as this sounds, the most common response of women about a man they can trust is that he does what he says

and says what he means. There is something quietly reassuring about a man who, when he tells you he'll call before dinner, actually picks up the phone and who, when he says he'll come by tomorrow night, actually shows up. Or if he doesn't, he has a good explanation.

Watch for a basic congruence between words and feelings and actions. For example, a man says he feels like you are the best thing since sliced bread. You hear the words, and he may be looking deeply into your eyes when he says them, but do his actions match his words? Does he treat you like a man would treat a woman he really cared for? You don't want to make the mistake of loving a man so much that you overlook a big disconnect between what he says, what he seems to feel, and what he does. Those three need to line up pretty consistently.

Can This Man Be Wrong?

It is amazing how much strength is communicated through the quality of humility and especially the absence of an ego that requires continual feeding.

> *It is amazing how much strength is communicated through the quality of humility.*

I once worked with a couple who had broken off their engagement shortly before the wedding. Within two weeks, the would-be groom knew he had made the mistake of his life. His wedding jitters had been little more, really, than an indicator of his need to grow up and take responsibility for loving a wonderful woman who had less of a pedigree than his family preferred. In the painful aftermath, he saw his mistake with crystal clarity. He did the hard work of deep personal change. He also put feet to his new understanding. With no one's prompting, he humbled himself enough to drive half a day to apologize to his ex-fiancée's parents and her family. This was his idea entirely—and a rather courageous one, since he knew he could meet with a door slammed on his nose. But when a man lets go of his pride, God gives him a kind of strength that is rooted in something larger than himself.

Later, his still ex-fiancée asked me, "Do you think I'd be the fool of the century to marry this man, given all we've been through?" A broken engagement had been a crushing disappointment for them both, yet they were still very much in love.

It was a totally understandable question. Any woman would think twice. "I think you are asking a deeper question about whether you can trust this man," I replied. And then I encouraged her to weigh the amount of change she saw in the man she loved, especially the humility he displayed in taking responsibility for his immaturity, and then to consider whether the humility led her to deeper trust.

Does He Enjoy You?

More telling than whether a man is attracted to you or likes your family or admires your career is his enjoyment of you. Your intuitive sense of being enjoyed tells you whether you can trust him. Does this man just plain *like* you for who you are? Your adventuresome spirit may be an irritation to some, or your quietness may be misunderstood by many, but this man enjoys those kind of things about you and sees in them real value and worth.

I asked a friend who is a great "idea woman," a lover of books, what sealed her affection for the man she married. Her response was telling. "He enjoyed my mind," she explained. He wasn't intimidated by her intelligence; he did not wish away her philosophical bent. She sensed she could trust this man with this crucial aspect of herself.

In the world of counseling, I have noticed that the question of "being enjoyed" is the one that most often brings a person to tears. "Does your father or your mother or a good friend or the man you married—or anyone on the planet—just plain enjoy you—as the unique and gifted, flawed and sometimes failing, woman you are?" Ask that question and be prepared to hand a woman a Kleenex. All of us long to feel that someone knows us deeply—and still loves us truly.

> *All of us long to feel that someone knows us deeply— and still loves us truly.*

Being enjoyed by someone is very close to feeling really loved, perhaps as close as we get in this life. That's why we long to take pleasure in God and for him to take pleasure in us. And we will always want this from any man to whom we give our hearts.

Can He Take Risks for the Sake of Love?

To love a woman well requires that a man move out of himself and his own frame of reference into territory that feels as uncharted to him as anything Lewis and Clark faced when they ventured into the great Northwest. A genuine relationship with a woman to whom he commits himself, body and soul, is at once incredibly attractive and mildly terrifying—though, of course, few men would admit it. In a committed relationship, a man will have to do battle with feelings of inadequacy that appear regularly and out of nowhere, it seems. Taking risks for the sake of love is what signals you that a man is willing to engage in this battle.

Cecelia's story helps illustrate this. Of all the men Cecelia ever dated, Joel, an insurance broker with a love of all things aesthetic—poetry, paintings, books, classic architecture—was the one with whom she felt the most instantaneous connection. Dating Joel, however, was like dancing in tandem with a phantom. He would call her when he came to town, take her out for expensive dinners, and genuinely marvel at her intuitive ability to see into his soul. "You rattle me to my toes, and I love that," he would say on occasion. Then he would disappear into a haze of work and travel, punctuated with warm and cozy emails. But nothing more. He would get close and then get scared—and then drop off the face of the earth.

Cecelia hung in there because she just plain liked the guy that much. He was a wonderful man in many respects, but he was content to sample only. He would get right up to the edge of making a commitment to a relationship he clearly valued—and then he would back away from taking the actual risk that love entails. One night over coffee and dessert, after his declarations of how much he enjoyed an evening in her charming company, she pointed out this pattern.

"You know, I feel like a treasured bottle of wine to you. And you're content to simply pour a glass and then put the bottle back in the rack until next time," she said as gently and truthfully as she knew.

The color of hot pink slowly crept into Joel's cheeks. Her comment made him mad. It blew his cover. He had never had a woman call him on a pattern of toying with her—of reeling her in emotionally and then running away. If Joel simply could have owned his struggle to take a risk, he might well have overcome it. But he moved the other way—back into the world of pretense and pretending. When Joel called back a year later, he was still looking merely for a tasty sample. This time Cecelia declined.

A man you can trust will have a different response. He may sweat bullets inside at the thought of giving himself to one woman, one relationship. Love is full of take-your-breath-away risks. But when the time comes to do battle with his fear, he will face it and move through it and become stronger in the process. He will not just string you along.

The Most Essential X-Ray

As I said earlier, we all wish for a machine that could x-ray a person's heart. It would make trust much easier. The Bible offers not an X-ray but a set of scales that weighs out the character of a man. It's like saying, "Don't move forward in a relationship in which these red flags are present." If you do, you'll find yourself skating on ice that is not strong enough to support you. The basis for trust will not be there.

If you have even a passing acquaintance with the Bible, you will have heard of the Proverbs 31 woman who represents the highest ideals a man could hope to find in any woman. What most of us miss are the first nine verses of chapter 31 that describe the man who is worthy of such a woman. Or you might say that these verses describe the essential starting points of what will become solid character in a man. Three characteristics in particular are pointed out here in the form of a mother's advice to her son.

1. "Do not spend your strength on women, your vigor on those who ruin kings."[82] In other words, beware of the man who is a womanizer—who needs the constant attention of a woman in order to function well. Look out for the man whose sense of

self is wrapped around some woman's ankles. Who can't be alone and without a relationship. Who measures himself by the gleam of approval he sees in her eyes—whoever she is. This tendency in men is so common that the first admonition out of this wise mother's mouth is, "Don't spend your strength on women." Even great men are destroyed this way. A man who gives his heart to God first will be able to love and serve a woman without being dependent on her. He is standing on his own two feet because he knows what it is to bow his knee and his will before God.

2. "It is not for kings . . . to drink wine, nor for rulers to crave beer, lest they drink . . . and deprive all the oppressed of their rights."[83] This is the scale of addiction. You can't build a lasting relationship with a person who is controlled by substance, because the addiction will control you both. Even a "king" will neglect to do the one thing he is most responsible for—to attend to the needs of the poor and the oppressed. Brought into the realm of a relationship, this is saying that you can't hope for much from a man who is overcome from within. As anyone who has ever been in love with someone in the grip of addiction will attest, it's like trying to hug a shadow.

You can't hope for much from a man who is overcome from within.

3. "Speak up for those who cannot speak for themselves, for the rights of all who are destitute. Speak up and judge fairly; defend the rights of the poor and needy."[84] This is the mother's one prescription, one positive teaching. She is telling her son something terribly important—how to use his strength as a

man. He is to be a man for others, a man to make things happen for those his influence touches.

Have you known a man who is far enough along to realize his potential influence—who wants his life to have an impact on others for good and for a cause larger than his own self-interests? Such a man will someday become like a huge oak tree whose roots are sunk deep and who provides shade and sustenance for many people. He knows he was put on the planet for more than his own pleasure—and you are the one who will most feel the benefit of this.

This last teaching gives crucial direction in discerning the kind of man you want to join your life with for the long haul. Simply put, has he moved beyond himself? Is he able to invite you to join him in something larger than either of you?

Real Vulnerability

So trust is the basis for a love that lasts and a relationship that can weather the storms of life. As Lynn and Jeff's story reveals, it takes time and a bit of a track record to know whether what you think you see in someone is truly there. (And it goes without saying that what you would hope to see in another, you need to be in the process of actually becoming.) Personally, I'm in favor of a good many cups of coffee—maybe enough to support one small local Starbucks near you.

What is happening as two people become a couple is like a prolonged card game—it takes awhile to share your cards with each other. You each have in your hand a big deck full of past, present, and future cards. This deck includes a lot of interesting stuff—like how you felt about going to a new high school your senior year and where you have been hurt and what scares you at 3:00 a.m. in the dark. Some of those cards have to do with the things you love and the experiences you hope never to repeat. Some cast way into the future—the hopes and dreams you may only be beginning to admit to yourself. A few cards are tattered and frayed and probably hidden behind other ones you think are "prettier." At some point in this fascinating interchange that takes place over weeks and months—or maybe a few years—all the cards you know in your hand (some you don't know yet) need to be laid on the table. The good, the bad, and the wish-it-had-never-happened.

This is the picture of vulnerability, which is the emotional fuel that empowers trust. The root of the word "vulnerability" is worth noting. It means "able to be wounded." It is the opposite of self-protection and the feeling that you always have to put your very best self forward. In the beginning of a relationship, the only self we can offer is our "best self," the one that has been most applauded in our past—our dazzling intellect, our stunning good looks, our deep spirituality. But it must go further; it must move into the places that feel more vulnerable. We may be met, not with applause and approval, but with the stale taste of rejection. That's the risk.

You will know that you love a man when you feel safe with him though the worst is known. And you will feel that you can trust each other when you sense that the best God has put in you is celebrated and truly enjoyed.

Vulnerability of the heart is always supposed to precede, by a long shot, vulnerability of the body, which is another euphemism for sex. It was such a gift to Lynn and Jeff, for instance, that sex was not allowed to preempt this far more intricate dance of getting to know each other. Sex didn't take over the card game.

It is a strange irony that sometimes it is *less vulnerable* to be sexually involved—to be two strangers in the night—than it is to share your life and your heart with someone. Real vulnerability followed by genuine commitment to a person makes sexual intimacy one of the best joys on earth. This sort of joy is simply not possible in a relationship that is not for keeps. As the opening quote by William May explains, we don't give ourselves to another fully if the future is withheld.

In the final analysis, a good relationship is not about the absence of vice. The celibacy of dating or courting or getting to know someone—all the precursors to marriage—is meant to clear out the space for the really important stuff to grow and flourish. You are planting a garden meant to last a lifetime. You are investing in a relationship that has to be nurtured and tended to all your days. In a good relationship, celibacy makes room for the practice of showing respect and honor to another, for the practice of self-giving that allows the two of you to be better together than you could ever be apart.

Seen from certain angles, this coming together of two people can look like loss and subtraction, as though the giving of oneself is a kind of death. Perhaps in some ways it is. But it is death that also leads to the experience of personal resurrection. In this union of two people, body and soul, the sum is truly greater than the parts—and the individuals themselves become somehow more who they truly are. In marriage there is a hint of something

In marriage there is a hint of something only God could dream up, something bigger than the two of you combined.

only God could dream up, something bigger than the two of you combined. Or as Frederick Buechner explains:

> By all the laws of both logic and simple arithmetic, to give yourself away in love to another would seem to mean that you end up with less of yourself left than you had to begin with. But the miracle is that just the reverse is true, logic and arithmetic go hang. To give yourself away in love to somebody else . . . is to become for the first time yourself fully. To live not just for yourself alone anymore but for another self to whom you swear to be true—plight your troth to, your truth to—is in a new way to come fully alive.[85]

Sexuality and Your Soul

1. Think through the men you have known. What has been true of the ones you felt you could trust?

2. How much a part of your life are the traits of humility, courage, freedom from addiction, and living for something larger than yourself? Which of those do you most want to see growth in—and why?

3. When have you felt enjoyed by a man for who you are, and how would you describe the experience? What kind of impact did it have on you?

4. When you think of genuine vulnerability with someone, which word most describes your gut response?
   Why?

   fear
   longing
   mistrust
   joy
   shame

5. In terms of what you felt and understood as you
   read this chapter, how would you evaluate any relationship you currently have with a man?

Chapter 11

The Making of a Man

Most men want the maiden without any sort of cost to themselves.

John Eldredge

For many a man, the most terrifying thing he can imagine is making a commitment to an equal, honest, intimate relationship with a woman.

Dr. Frank Pittman

$\mathcal{O}$ur discussion of sexuality would be incomplete without looking at the question from a man's vantage point. From all observations, it would appear to be a great time to be a guy. Sex has never been more readily available. And not just sex with one woman whom a man has to jump through hoops to please, but sex with a variety of women who may ask little of him at all. You would think that men would be high-fiving each other on every street corner.

The age-old, acquired skill of learning how to court a woman—to woo and romance her with no guarantee of anything in return—has almost disappeared from the scene, leaving an unnamed ache in all of us. Courting a woman is an ancient rite of passage that helped turn a boy into a man you could lean on, expect something of, and trust with your life. We are all—men and women—suffering because of its waning influence.

When I talk to younger women, I often find they feel a tad guilty at the thought of denying sexual favor in its many and varied forms to a man—as though it is just too hard on him to expect that kind of restraint. And of course, there is always the fear that he'll turn elsewhere for sexual intimacy. Such guilt and fear, though, reveals how little most women understand about the way men come to be real men—and the unrivaled role we play in this process.

Growing Up Male

When Ted looks back on his twenties, he sees how lost he was in terms of relating to women. His immigrant father was a man with a quick temper who didn't know much about the tender parts of love. "Having a girlfriend was about making myself feel good," Ted admits, a tad sheepishly. "If this woman could make me happy, I was in the relationship. And if she couldn't, it was over. Most of my twenties was about *me*."

Ted also admits that he struggled with Internet porn for a few years. The fantasy of a woman who seemed to offer an unending supply of affection hooked him. This screen-sized woman wanted him, and she never, ever made him feel rejected. It was so easy—too easy. Pornography sapped him of his spiritual strength, turning his relationship with God into a pile of mush that left him going through life in a lethargic, unmotivated haze. He felt like a man trying to climb a rocky mountain on stilts.

Knowing that he was now, at the age of thirty-five, engaged to a great woman, I asked him how this transformation occurred. His response says a lot about the way a man moves from his own self-centeredness to being able to care for others—to love and shelter and lead them in the ways that men do best. "I eventually got very tired of feeling ensnared by these images of women—all the while being powerless to actually relate to one of them well. Honestly, a real longing for holiness came into my life. I wanted, more than anything, to be a man of integrity before God. And I began to ask—beg—God for my freedom."

Ted gained this freedom bit by solid bit and found in the process that his passion was dammed up into a reservoir of courage and initiative that enlivened every part of his life. His career took off—his mental fog cleared. "A verse in Proverbs describes what happened in my life," Ted says, going on to quote how the wicked person flees in the face of challenge but the righteous man is "as bold as a lion."[86] Ted began to experience this boldness. He had the strength to tackle things that had easily defeated him before.

Within a year or so, Ted met an interesting woman, and what caught his attention was the change in his own heart. "When I met Kristy," he says, "I had an overwhelming desire to love this woman well. I remember thinking how different it felt—to want to love and serve and give to a woman."

Contrary to other accounts, I am convinced that there are good numbers of "Teds" out there, men who would echo his words. And more than anything, they need women in their lives who insist that they offer nothing less than they are capable of offering—a heart to love and serve and give to a woman and to the family they create together.

"I had an overwhelming desire to love ... and serve and give to a woman."

Ted's life is a window into the struggle of growing up male in our culture. For years now, men have felt the sting of shame attached to their masculinity—as though their maleness badly needed to be domesticated. Classic male traits are often treated these days as pathology to be cured. Boys are too active in class, so we give them Ritalin. They play with guns, and we call it aggressive. They are big and loud and competitive, and it's a problem to be solved. Only lust—as in a constant desire to make it with a woman—is allowable, even expected of a true red-blooded male. As long as rape and pillage are not part of the picture, simple lust is seen as masculine—desired and highly prized. For many men, it is the only way they know to feel like a man.

A man's struggle here is crucial to understand. His masculinity is not a given to him. It is, in fact, much harder to feel secure in his maleness than it is for a woman to feel validated as a woman. "Do I have what it takes? Am I man enough?" These are the kinds of questions a man brings into any arena he enters—athletic competition, the corner office, the bedroom, or the battlefield. Can he meet the challenge? Being a man is more like a prize to be won, to be fought for in "small battles of honor"[87] and proving oneself.

Avoiding the Easiest Route

I offer the preceding as backdrop to the discussion of how celibacy outside of marriage is actually the making of a man. The easiest and most sure way to feel like a man is to have sex. It is the quickest feedback loop, a deep physical dose of masculine validation. The experience of sexual virility is so potent for a guy that his lifelong temptation is to turn it into a god and to make the woman the center of his existence rather than a person herself and his partner.

Have you ever had a man try to make you the sun in his universe? It feels pretty good for a while—but only for a while. Then it starts to grow old because too much is hanging on you. Your words are too important, your presence too necessary. As

John Eldredge notes in his book about men, *Wild at Heart*, most women would prefer to accompany a man on the adventure of life; they do not want to be the adventure itself.

When a man gets his sexuality confused with his soul, his actual self, he succumbs to what poet Robert Bly called "the myth of the Golden-Haired Woman."[88] Somewhere out there is a woman larger than life, the perfect soul mate, whose love and affection will make him a man. Think of all the movies built around this theme! Until he can break through this mirage, no ordinary woman will ever be enough. He will move from woman to woman, girlfriend to girlfriend, captured by the myth that the next woman can bestow on him the ultimate validation of himself as a man. Bly describes the illusion:

> He sees a woman across the room, knows immediately that it is "She." He drops the relationship he has, pursues her, feels wild excitement, passion, beating heart, obsession. After a few months, everything collapses; she becomes an ordinary woman. He is confused and puzzled. Then he sees once more a radiant face across the room, and the old certainty comes again.[89]

It's as though, in some way, every man remembers Eve. As John Eldredge puts it, "We are haunted by her. And somehow we believe that if we could find her, get her back, then we'd also recover with her our own lost masculinity."[90] This is the longing that fuels the myth for a man.

The problem comes when a man brings his quest for validation to you—or to any woman. Sexual intimacy is the easiest and quickest route he knows, but to go there is only to deepen the illusion that a woman's love is the salve of his soul. It is not.

Femininity can never confer masculinity. He must find his own rootedness as a man in the one who made him and in the company of other men. As Eldredge says so well, "The masculine journey always takes a man *away* from the woman, in order that he may come back to her with his question answered. A man does not go to a woman to get his strength; he goes to her to *offer* it."[91]

What a fundamental shift! It is so different to have a man approach you out of the desire to offer his strength to you. He is free to look out for your interests as well as his own. And if he is really concerned about you, the last thing he wants to do is jeopardize your sexual integrity.

Once in the early days of knowing my husband, Stacy, when we were just two friends riding in a car pool to work in Birmingham, another guy (in the same car pool) touched me in a subtle but oddly inappropriate way. I shrugged it off as a fluke moment. Without a word from me, Stacy took the initiative to pull this guy aside later and talk to him about it. "What were you thinking? Didn't you realize the way you touched Paula was a bit off?" he asked. I was stunned. I had never had a man "fight for my honor." And it felt surprisingly good.

> *He loves you because this is what he was made to do— this is what a real man does.*

When a man is not dependent on you for validation, he sees you differently. You are not the mirror of his worth. Your affection is not the ego stroke he rests upon. He does not feel required to keep you happy or to make your life a bed of roses so that his life will be one. He loves you because this is what he was made to do—this is what a real man does. The joy comes, as Ted said, in being able to offer himself.

What Celibacy Does for a Man

Allowing a man to enjoy sexual favor without having to take the risk of real commitment in marriage invites him to remain a boy inside. A recent national survey to discover why men won't commit to marriage as easily these days illustrates well how promiscuity permits men to get stuck as perpetual adolescents. These are the top reasons men gave for preferring to cohabit with a romantic partner—and why, if women will let them, they prefer to audition for marriage rather than take the manly leap.[92]

- They had the convenience of a regular sex partner they did not have to search for—she was just there waiting.
- There was someone to take care of the house and the dog when he was away.
- He felt "less answerable to a partner"; he could come and go as he pleased.
- His financial assets were better protected.
- A live-in girlfriend was his "best option for now," allowing him time to look for the ideal soul mate.

Do you hear the self-centeredness in these reasons men gave for preferring cohabitation to marriage? (Certainly, mere logic does not favor cohabitation as a preview to marriage, as the marriages that emerge from living together are less likely to succeed.) Sexual favor before marriage simply stunts the growth of boys into real men who can shoulder the responsibility of others because they have moved outside the narrow confines of their own immediate needs.

In the best of ways, celibacy causes the damming up of a man's strength and vitality. It forces him to deal with himself. He has to do battle with his sexuality—to ride it like a wild stallion until its power is harnessed and under his control. Then he gets the great gift of being able to use his sexuality for a larger purpose. This is the reasoning behind the verse often quoted in this regard: "For this is the will of God, your sanctification; that is, that you abstain from sexual immorality; that each of you know how to possess his own vessel in sanctification and honor, not in lustful passion."[93]

Don't you love that phrase—"to possess his own vessel"? (Try that on the next man who comes on to you: "Honey, you just need to possess your own vessel.") However antiquated the words, the imagery is important here. Possessing one's own vessel speaks of a man's need to be the captain of his own ship if he ever intends to sail the high seas or carry the lives and cargo of others with him.

While it is true that men who can find a good supply of women to bed seem to swagger with confidence, their inner lives are another thing altogether. The promiscuous man knows inside that his strength is being dissipated. He is Samson with his hair cut. His virility is confined to the four corners of a bed when it is meant, quite literally, to change the world.

While it is true that men who can find a good supply of women to bed seem to swagger with confidence, their inner lives are another thing altogether.

Having to actually court a woman is something no man should be allowed to miss. Does it strike you what a gift it is to a guy when *he* has to be the one to pursue you? Men become men by doing battle with their fears, and pursuing a woman well is a process filled with man-sized risks. He must cross the floor to ask you to dance at thirteen. He picks up the phone a few years later, braced for the sound of rejection or reception in your voice. On and on the dance goes until one day he must gather the courage to stake his whole future on asking you to be his wife.

At every juncture, a man feels naked and fearfully exposed, braced for the turndown. But that's the nature of fear; it only subsides when you walk straight into it. To grow up inside, a man must get past his fear of Woman. For as we all know, we come to hate the things we fear. How can a man ever love you well if he is still so afraid of your rejection?

One man who built custom homes for a living explained to me how leaving the world of the sexually illicit helped him overcome his fears. He said, "I finally realized all this mingling and tingling kept me from actually *feeling my need* of a woman long enough to do something about it—like make an intentional, gutsy move toward one woman in particular." Indeed, making this move toward a woman-in-particular is the point. A man walks into the fire without the blanket of sexual affirmation around him, and he does the thing a man is supposed to do: He pursues a woman to know her in this larger, fuller sense with absolutely no expectation that he will be rewarded with physical intimacy.

It is by such means that men become men.

God and Men

As a woman, I take my cues—which is to say that I learn a lot—by watching the way God addresses a man. I have already alluded to the straightforward instructions God gives a man about his sexuality: "Possess your own vessel . . . in honor." Indeed, sexuality is the place God begins with a man. The first rite in the Jewish tradition is the act of circumcision, eight days after a boy's birth. A fascinating piece of history lies behind this requirement.

In the pagan culture that surrounded the Hebrew religion, male sexuality controlled the culture. In our language we would say, "It was a zoo." There were no boundaries. Sex and worship were joined—a man could worship his god by having sex with a temple prostitute. Homosexuality among Greek men was rampant. Indeed, a common expression was "A man for pleasure, a woman for babies." Women existed as objects of male gratification in whatever form. They were hardly more than chattel.

Follow with me the staggering intervention of God into this hedonistic world. God called the Hebrews to be his chosen people, and he drew a firm boundary around sexuality, corralling its powerful forces to the enjoyment of one man and one woman for a lifetime—a union from which new life comes in the form of children and grandchildren to care for. (Remember that a man could not be conscripted for the army during the first year of marriage because bringing pleasure to his wife was literally his job description.) While polygamy was rampant throughout the Old Testament, it was never God's intention, and it worked about as poorly as one would expect!

From a Hebrew boy's earliest days, then, his sexuality was marked by the touch of God on his life. In circumcision, his very flesh was cut. Daily he had the most graphic reminder possible that his sexuality was, first of all, a matter of covenant between God and him. When he saw his own flesh, he remembered to whom he belonged.

The intervention of God into the lusts and desires of men not only allowed for the creation of culture, it established the basis by which a woman is to be cherished by a man. No longer could a man covet his neighbor's wife and get away with it. He could not enjoy a woman's sexual favor and then write her out a certificate of divorce when he found a younger version. A woman was to be honored as a lifelong partner. This "honoring" goes even further in the New Testament. There a husband is told that his wife is an equal partner sexually and that he is required to meet *her* sexual needs![94] He is called to love her sacrificially, "as Christ loved the church and gave himself up for her."[95] Furthermore, his prayers will tend to bounce off heaven if he does not live with his wife in an understanding way.[96]

Does this give you a better idea of the radical way in which God does business with a man and his sexuality?

A fascinating encounter between God and Job speaks volumes about how God views manhood. Job has lost everything—his children, his fortune, his health. He wishes he had never been born. He wonders how this has happened to him, a man who has lived a righteous life. His friends weigh in with their pathetic opinions. And then God speaks. Words of empathy and commiseration are not what God offers. Listen in on the particular kind of "comfort" God offers this tormented man:

> "Who is this that darkens my counsel
> with words without knowledge?
> Brace yourself like a man;
> I will question you,
> and you shall answer me.

Where were you when I laid the earth's foundation?
    Tell me, if you understand."[97]

Does this sound harsh? God looks at Job in his misery and says the equivalent of, "Stand up and talk to me like a man." I believe God is here offering Job the greatest compliment he could give him. God is speaking to a man who thinks he has lost everything. And God tells him, in effect, that he has not lost the most essential thing of all. Job is invited to stand before the living God—as a man.

This is why it is a travesty for a man to rest his sense of self on you, a woman. Being a man is something God *bestows*—he gives innately as a good father would. No woman can take this away from a man unless he invests that kind of power and idolatry in her. And a woman cannot confer masculinity on a man no matter how many times she sleeps with him. All God allows either gender is to give witness to that which he has already done in the other.

> *It is a travesty for a man to rest his sense of self on you, a woman.*

The Farmer Takes a Wife

Do you remember the nursery rhyme you sang as a child? "The farmer takes a wife, the farmer takes a wife, hi-ho, the derrio, the farmer takes a wife." It sounds like perhaps he has purchased her at the market, but the actual meaning behind the rhyme says something far more. It speaks of the huge responsibility a man takes on when he joins his life with a woman in marriage. I offer the story of an actual couple by way of illustration.

John loved the summer he spent with Alice working in the mountains of North Carolina. She was willing to come to his hometown to serve tables at a local resort. Her grandmother lived conveniently nearby, so she had a place to stay. Nearly every night John and Alice found their own entertainment in the concerts and art shows and theater venues that fill the warm nights of a vacation destination. It's not like they really needed "entertaining," for John was quite happy just simply being with Alice. It mattered little to him what they did.

Their summer together was the climax to a year or so of long-distance phone calls and occasional weekend visits. By the time the summer ended, their relationship had come to a fork in the road, and John felt this reality the most. As the autumn leaves began to turn their first colors, an odd malaise settled in on him. Where should this relationship go? Was marriage the place where this was all headed, and how did he feel about it? Was he ready to take this on? John knew, in the truest sense of the expression, the ball was in his court. He and Alice could not continue to get closer and more attached unless their relationship was going somewhere. That would not be fair.

I watched John wrestle with this essentially male rite of passage and recognized, perhaps for the first time, what steps toward marriage feel like for a man. A man knows, deep in his gut, that he is truly taking on the responsibility of other lives in a whole new way. As one man shared insightfully, "A woman dies to herself—her dreams and her agenda—when she has children. But a man does when he takes a wife."

It is important for us as women to appreciate what love and courtship and marriage mean for a man—what he invests, the fears he must overcome, the joys he experiences. Otherwise, we may miss this sweet death he dies. We may not recognize the doors to relationship and deep connection that we are privileged to open in him.

Perhaps you remember the true story, told in the movie *Anna and the King*, about a widowed schoolteacher and her son who have come to teach the children of the king of Siam. She has a whole classroom of children to teach because the king has a number of concubines—no wife, but plenty of women in his life, since polygamy is the common practice of the monarchy. (What we see now in serial relationships with no lasting attachment isn't all that different.)

The king makes the mistake of falling in love with his children's widowed schoolteacher. He is angry with himself, for he has upset the order of his own kingdom. He is accustomed to having the affection of women who serve him at his beck and call. But he has never had a relationship with one—not until Anna. In a scene where the two of them are dancing outside his palace, looking out over the ocean, the king utters a line that could be echoed by men throughout the ages. He says, "I didn't know there was so much to be had in the love of one woman."

You are capable of inviting a man into a relationship so deep and valuable that it is worth the reordering of his entire life.

That's the secret you possess. You are capable of inviting a man into a relationship so deep and valuable that it is worth the reordering of his entire life. There is so much to be had in the love of one woman—there is so much to be had in your love. You have such a good gift to offer the right man that it must not be squandered. It means too much.

You are designed to usher a man, through the door of his sexuality, into another world relationally, one that will provide him the richest dividends of his life—children, family, deep connection to others, posterity. Finally, his sexuality will become fruitful in ways better than he could have imagined. In his real and lasting attachment to one woman, he sheds the empty freedom of his bachelor state. For you, he will leave behind his trivial pursuits. You are the prize, and your love is worth the death he must die.

Most of us women, when we know the worth of what we have to bring to a man, will guard it with our lives. It is the treasure God put in you. He himself cups his hands around it like a light that flickers in the darkness. Whatever has happened in your life—nevertheless, the light burns steadily on.

And even the darkness is not able to overcome it.

Sexuality and Your Soul

1. What kind of insight did this chapter give you into the particular challenges of growing up male?

2. How do you feel when a guy makes you "too important" in his life?

3. How would you describe a relationship in which a man is offering his strength to you rather than trying to gain his validation from you?

4. How would you discern that a man is indeed overcoming his own set of fears—regarding you, regarding life? What do you see as key to this?

5. What do you learn about men from the way God deals with a man?

Afterword

I hope you have found the material in this book helpful in your own journey. Confronting the questions and exploring the longings that lie at the root of your sexuality is not easy work, but it tends to be very fruitful—all the more so because it touches so many parts of your life. It has the potential to shape the way you think of yourself and how you relate to a man. And most especially, it is an incredibly powerful avenue by which you come to know God and to be known by him.

As you finish this book I leave you with a verse I have come to love:

> And let the beauty of the LORD our God be upon us,
>   And establish the work of our hands for us;
>   Yes, establish the work of our hands.[98]

Acknowledgments

This book is not one I dreamed of writing. None of my wistful lists of lifetime goals include an entry of authoring a book about sex. Somehow I stumbled into writing this book—ironically, with more fervor and passion than anything I have ever written. Literally compelled to write about women and sexuality, I was gripped by the subject from start to finish. It was as though I'd been carried out to sea on a huge wave and kept there for months, rowing and rowing.

I should first thank Dr. Paul and Shirley Simms of Purdue University for an invitation to speak at a large college gathering there that awakened in me the desire to explore the sexual scene as so many younger women find it these days. During this time, my daughter, Allison, a great joy in my life, was finishing her undergraduate work at the University of North Carolina at Chapel Hill, where she had joined my old college sorority. From the stories she brought home, I was initially startled at how much had changed in twenty-five years. The hook-up scene, the casualness with which men and women serviced each other sexually, the waning of romance and of the pleasure of being pursued by a man for something other than sex—these struck a deep note of grief in me that eventually translated into study and prayer and finally writing.

I cannot begin to thank the women who have shared their stories with me in the context of a private counseling practice here in Raleigh and those who have poured out their tales after I've spoken in a seminar or conference elsewhere. I am grateful for your honesty and for the privilege of having a small part in the reclamation of your hearts. Please know that I've tried to preserve the integrity of your stories while disguising the source.

Many people have had a hand in bringing this book to completion. To Linda Glasford, Greg Johnson, and Sandra Vander Zicht, my special thanks for believing in this book from the start. To the marketing team at Zondervan so willing to brainstorm the title and the packaging of an idea into an attractive form, I am grateful. My thanks to Leanne Payne and the Pastoral Care Ministries Team for opening up my understanding of the freedom of repentance and the life the gospel is meant to bring us. I am grateful to Myra Hodges and many others for their peek into the past. Connally Gillam has supplied great stories and much insight; I am truly in her debt. Sally Breedlove has been my own personal Bible consultant, always available with a fresh idea solidly rooted in truth. And finally, this book would not exist in this form without the faithfulness of a small team of people who have prayed regularly for this effort and for the women who will read it. My deep gratitude to Jennifer Ennis, Edith Struick, Dianne Gorsuch, Carol Taylor, Jan Shacklett, Ruth Brooks, and Clyde and MaryLynne Hodson, as well as a host of women scattered hither and yon who are concerned for the relational world a generation of younger women are inheriting from us. May God reward you, truly.

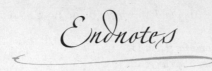

Endnotes

1. John 8:34–36 TNIV.
2. Wendy Shalit, *A Return to Modesty* (New York: Simon & Schuster, 1999), 209.
3. Wendy Shalit's appropriate phrase.
4. Danielle Crittenden, *What Our Mothers Didn't Tell Us* (New York: Simon & Schuster, 1999), 39.
5. Brain imaging studies also show that structurally women have a larger deep limbic system than men, which makes them more in touch with their feelings and gives them a greater capacity to bond with others. See Dr. Daniel Amen's work in *Change Your Brain, Change Your Life* (New York: Three Rivers Press, 1998).
6. Barbara Dafoe Whitehead, *Why There Are No Good Men Left* (New York: Broadway Books, 2003), 31.
7. Crittenden, *What Our Mothers Didn't Tell Us*, 31.
8. Shalit, *A Return to Modesty*, 34.
9. Shalit, *A Return to Modesty*, 34.
10. Cited in Andrew Morton, *Madonna* (New York: St. Martin's Press, 2001), 21.
11. For a fuller understanding of sexuality before and after the infusion of Judeo-Christian values, see Mario Bergman's *Setting Love in Order* (Grand Rapids: Baker, 1995), and Dennis Prager's *Think a Second Time* (New York: HarperCollins, 1996).
12. Shalit, *A Return to Modesty*, 88 (emphasis mine).
13. Stephen Ambrose, *D-Day* (New York: Random House, 1993), 557.
14. Genesis 1:26–27 NLT (emphasis mine).
15. See Isaiah 49:15.
16. John Eldredge, *Wild at Heart* (Nashville: Nelson), 182.
17. Mike Mason, *The Mystery of Marriage* (Portland, Ore.: Multnomah, 1985), 111.
18. Shalit, *A Return to Modesty*, 98.

19. George Gilder, *Men and Marriage* (Baton Rouge, La.: Pelican Books, 1983), 5.

20. Gilder, *Men and Marriage*, 11.

21. Gilder, *Men and Marriage*, 12.

22. See Proverbs 6:25–29.

23. Wendy Shalit's descriptive phrase.

24. Deuteronomy 24:5.

25. Proverbs 22:28.

26. C. S. Lewis used the apt term "chronological snobbery" to describe the bias that our time in history is somehow the brightest time.

27. Naomi Wolf, *Promiscuities* (New York: Random House, 1997), 119–36.

28. Mary Pipher, *Reviving Ophelia* (New York: Ballantine, 1994), 19.

29. See Shalit, *A Return to Modesty*, 105.

30. Shalit, *A Return to Modesty*, 209 (emphasis mine).

31. John 10:10, emphasis mine.

32. Ephesians 5:27.

33. Proverbs 30:18–19, emphasis mine.

34. Crittenden, *What Our Mothers Didn't Tell Us*, 36.

35. Shalit, *A Return to Modesty*, 147.

36. See John 8:1–11.

37. John 8:7 TNIV.

38. John 8:10–11.

39. Frederick Buechner, *Whistling in the Dark* (San Francisco: HarperSanFrancisco, 1993), 78–79.

40. Lisa Bevere, *Kissed the Girls and Made Them Cry* (Nashville: Nelson, 2002), 77.

41. Genesis 2:24 NASB.

42. John Eldredge, *The Journey of Desire* (Nashville: Nelson, 2000), 126.

43. Song of Songs 5:1–2.

44. Genesis 24:66–67.

45. Hebrews 13:4.

46. Andy Crouch, ed., *Re:Generation Quarterly* 8, no. 2 (2003): 4.

47. Heard in a television interview with Harrison's sister days after his death.

48. Heard in a presentation given by Leanne Payne, Pastoral Care Ministries.

49. 1 Corinthians 6:18–19 TNIV.

50. Mason, *The Mystery of Marriage*, 122.

51. Zephaniah 3:17 NASB.

52. Eldredge, *The Journey of Desire*, 128.

53. Ephesians 5:31–32.
54. John Donne, "Holy Sonnet 14."
55. Pamela Rowen-Herzog, "Dialogue," Circle of Hope Church, Philadelphia, Pennsylvania (2001). Used by permission.
56. Bevere, *Kissed the Girls and Made Them Cry*, 122.
57. Mike Long, a public school health educator, seems to have coined this descriptive phrase. See his book *Parents: Everyone Is Not Doing It* (Ottawa, Ill.: Jameson Books, 2000).
58. Ephesians 1:18–19, emphasis mine.
59. For insightful help, see Elmer Towns, *Fasting for Spiritual Breakthrough* (Ventura, Calif.: Regal, 1990).
60. Isaiah 58:6.
61. Hebrews 4:15–16.
62. See Galatians 3:13–14.
63. Isaiah 30:18, emphasis mine.
64. John 8:31.
65. James 5:16.
66. Malachi 4:2.
67. "Valley of Achor" means "valley of trouble" and invokes the memory of some of Israel's most flagrant sin (see Joshua 7:26).
68. Hosea 2:14–15.
69. Isaiah 48:17.
70. Psalm 27:10 NASB.
71. Robin Norwood, *Women Who Love Too Much* (New York: Pocket Books, 1986), 40.
72. John 13:23.
73. Song of Songs 3:5.
74. See Lisa Bevere's book *Kissed the Girls and Made Them Cry* for an excellent discussion of this.
75. Bevere, *Kissed the Girls and Made Them Cry*, 129.
76. It's worth noting that the words "healthy" and "holy" both come from the same Anglo-Saxon root, *halig*.
77. See 1 Timothy 2:22.
78. See Proverbs 2:16; 5:3; 6:32.
79. Told by Connally Gillam. Used with permission.
80. Ronald Rolheiser, *The Holy Longing* (New York: Doubleday, 1999), 193.
81. Rolheiser, *The Holy Longing*, 192.
82. Proverbs 31:3.

83. Proverbs 31:4–5.

84. Proverbs 31:8–9.

85. Frederick Buechner, *A Room to Remember* (San Francisco: Harper SanFrancisco, 1984), 68–69.

86. Proverbs 28:1.

87. A concept further explored in Frank Pittman's insightful book *Man Enough* (New York: Perigee, 1993).

88. Robert Bly, *Iron John* (Reading, Mass.: Addison-Wesley, 1990), 135.

89. Bly, *Iron John*, 136.

90. Eldredge, *Wild at Heart*, 91.

91. Eldredge, *Wild at Heart*, 115.

92. Cited in "Why Men Won't Commit," in Barbara Dafoe Whitehead and David Popenoe, "The State of Our Unions: The Social Health of Marriage in America" (a 2002 study commissioned by The National Marriage Project).

93. 1 Thessalonians 4:3–5 NASB.

94. See 1 Corinthians 7:5.

95. Ephesians 5:25.

96. See 1 Peter 3:7.

97. Job 38:2–4.

98. Psalm 90:17 NKJV.

About the Author

Paula Rinehart is an author and counselor whose great pleasure is helping women understand the deeper issues of their hearts in the light of God's love and truth.

She is the author of *Strong Women, Soft Hearts* and the award-winning best seller *Choices,* which she wrote with her husband. Her articles have appeared in *Christianity Today, Marriage Partnership,* and *Discipleship Journal.* Paula and her husband ministered for many years on staff with The Navigators with college students and career singles. They live in Raleigh, North Carolina, where Paula maintains a private counseling practice. She also speaks to college groups and women's groups around the country on the topics of sexuality, relationships, and intimacy with God.

To contact Paula about women's conferences, seminars, and retreats, email her at paula@paularinehart.com or email Speak Up Speaker Services at speakupinc@aol.com; link to her website from: www.zondervan.com/author/RinehartP.

We want to hear from you. Please send your comments about this
book to us in care of zreview@zondervan.com. Thank you.

GRAND RAPIDS, MICHIGAN 49530 USA

WWW.ZONDERVAN.COM